CONTENTS

MW00571093

Multiply by 0 and 1 2
Match Multiplication to Addition: Facts for 2 3
Two Times Table 4
Match Multiplication to Addition: Facts for 3 6
Three Times Table 7
Multiply by 1, 2, and 3 9
Math Riddle: Multiplication Facts for 1, 2, and 3 . 10
Match Multiplication to Addition: Facts for 4 . . . 11
Four Times Table 12
Match Multiplication to Addition: Facts for 5 . . . 14
Five Times Table. 15
Match Multiplication to Addition: Facts for 6 . . . 17
Six Times Table 18
Multiply by 4, 5, and 6 20
Math Riddle: Multiplication Facts for 4, 5, and 6 . . 21
Match Multiplication to Addition: Facts for 7 . . . 22
Seven Times Table 23
Match Multiplication to Addition: Facts for 8 . . . 25
Eight Times Table 26
Match Multiplication to Addition: Facts for 9 . . . 28
Nine Times Table 29
Multiply by 7, 8, and 9 31
Math Riddle: Multiplication Facts for 7, 8, and 9 . . 32
Match Multiplication to Addition: Facts for 10 . . 33
Ten Times Table 34
Math Riddle: Multiplication Facts from 1 to 10 . . 36
Match Multiplication to Addition: Facts for 11 . . 37
Eleven Times Table 38
Match Multiplication to Addition: Facts for 12 . . 40
Twelve Times Table. 41
Multiply by 10, 11, and 12. 43
Math Riddle: Multiplication Facts for
    10, 11, and 12. 44
Math Blaster—Multiplication Challenge 1 45
Math Blaster—Multiplication Challenge 2 46
Math Blaster—Multiplication Challenge 3 47
Math Blaster—Multiplication Challenge 4 48
Math Blaster—Multiplication Challenge 5 49
Math Blaster—Multiplying by 1 to 6 50
Math Blaster—Multiplying by 7 to 12 55
Math Blaster—Multiplying by 1 to 12 60
Multiply by Tens 65
Multiply by Hundreds 66
Multiply by Thousands 67
Multiply Multiples of 10, 100, and 1000 68
Multiply Two-digit Numbers by
    One-digit Numbers 70
Multiply Multi-digit Numbers 75
Multiply Multi-digit Numbers—Challenge 1 76
Multiply Multi-digit Numbers—Challenge 2 77
Multiply Multi-digit Numbers—Challenge 3 78
Multiply Multi-digit Numbers—Challenge 4 79
Multiply Multi-digit Numbers—Challenge 5 80
Multiplication by 10, 100, and 1000—
    Challenge 1 81
Multiplication by 10, 100, and 1000—
    Challenge 2 82
Multiplication by 10, 100, and 1000—
    Challenge 3 83
Multiplication by 10, 100, and 1000—
    Challenge 4 84
Multiplication by 10, 100, and 1000—
    Challenge 5 85
How Am I Doing? 86
Multiplication Table for 0 to 12 89

Certificate of Merit—Multiplication 90
Answers 91

Multiply by 0 and 1

The product is always the same as the greater factor when any number is multiplied by 1. For example, $10 \times 1 = 10$.	The product is always 0 when any factor is multiplied by 0. For example, $0 \times 4 = 0$.

Multiply.

$0 \times 3 =$ _____	$2 \times 1 =$ _____	$8 \times 1 =$ _____	$0 \times 5 =$ _____
$3 \times 1 =$ _____	$0 \times 8 =$ _____	$5 \times 1 =$ _____	$7 \times 1 =$ _____
$0 \times 12 =$ _____	$11 \times 1 =$ _____	$0 \times 6 =$ _____	$6 \times 1 =$ _____
$4 \times 1 =$ _____	$0 \times 7 =$ _____	$9 \times 1 =$ _____	$0 \times 1 =$ _____
$0 \times 2 =$ _____	$1 \times 1 =$ _____	$0 \times 9 =$ _____	$12 \times 1 =$ _____

Match Multiplication to Addition: Facts for 2

Complete the multiplication facts for 2. Use a multiplication table to help you. Then write the sums. Underline each matching sum and product. Use a different colour for each pair.

1 × 2 = _____   2 + 2 + 2 + 2 + 2 = _____

2 × 2 = _____   2 + 2 + 2 + 2 + 2 + 2 + 2 + 2 + 2 + 2 + 2 + 2 = _____

3 × 2 = _____   2 + 0 = _____

4 × 2 = _____   2 + 2 + 2 + 2 + 2 + 2 + 2 + 2 + 2 + 2 = _____

5 × 2 = _____   2 + 2 + 2 + 2 + 2 + 2 + 2 = _____

6 × 2 = _____   2 + 2 + 2 + 2 + 2 + 2 + 2 + 2 = _____

7 × 2 = _____   2 + 2 + 2 = _____

8 × 2 = _____   2 + 2 = _____

9 × 2 = _____   2 + 2 + 2 + 2 = _____

10 × 2 = _____   2 + 2 + 2 + 2 + 2 + 2 + 2 + 2 + 2 = _____

11 × 2 = _____   2 + 2 + 2 + 2 + 2 + 2 + 2 + 2 + 2 + 2 + 2 = _____

12 × 2 = _____   2 + 2 + 2 + 2 + 2 + 2 = _____

Two Times Table

1. Multiply. Use the key to colour the products.

Colour Key
0 - red
2 - orange
4 - yellow
6 - green
8 - light blue
10 - dark blue
12 - purple
14 - pink
16 - brown
18 - grey
20 - black
22 - gold

7 × 2	0 × 2	3 × 2	8 × 2	5 × 2
6 × 2	2 × 2	11 × 2	9 × 2	4 × 2
1 × 2	2 × 3	12 × 2	2 × 7	2 × 4	2 × 9
2 × 10	2 × 6	2 × 11	2 × 0	2 × 12	2 × 5
2 × 8	2 × 1			

Tip for Multiplying by 2
Double the number!
For example, 4 × 2.
Think: 4 + 4 = 8. So 4 × 2 = 8.

Remember to practice skip counting by 2s!

2. Find the product.

A	E	I	M	N
8 × 2 = ____	5 × 2 = ____	11 × 2 = ____	0 × 2 = ____	12 × 2 = ____

O	P	S	T	X
1 × 2 = ____	4 × 2 = ____	10 × 2 = ____	2 × 2 = ____	7 × 2 = ____

Math Riddle: **What do you call a fake noodle?**

___ ___ / ___ ___ ___ ___ ___ ___ ___ !
16 24   22 0   8   16 20 4   16

3. Find the missing factor.

2 × ___ = 12	___ × 2 = 2	2 × ___ = 18	___ × 2 = 14
___ × 2 = 16	2 × ___ = 22	___ × 2 = 10	2 × ___ = 24
10 × ___ = 20	___ × 2 = 8	2 × ___ = 14	___ × 2 = 6
2 × ___ = 10	2 × ___ = 20	___ × 2 = 4	___ × 2 = 0

Match Multiplication to Addition: Facts for 3

Complete the multiplication facts for 3. Use a multiplication table to help you. Then write the sums. Underline each matching sum and product. Use a different colour for each pair.

$1 \times 3 =$ _____

$3 + 3 =$ _____

$2 \times 3 =$ _____

$3 + 3 + 3 + 3 + 3 + 3 =$ _____

$3 \times 3 =$ _____

$3 + 3 + 3 + 3 + 3 + 3 + 3 + 3 + 3 + 3 + 3 + 3 =$ _____

$4 \times 3 =$ _____

$3 + 3 + 3 =$ _____

$5 \times 3 =$ _____

$3 + 3 + 3 + 3 + 3 + 3 + 3 + 3 + 3 + 3 =$ _____

$6 \times 3 =$ _____

$3 + 3 + 3 + 3 + 3 + 3 + 3 + 3 =$ _____

$7 \times 3 =$ _____

$3 + 3 + 3 + 3 + 3 + 3 + 3 + 3 + 3 + 3 + 3 =$ _____

$8 \times 3 =$ _____

$3 + 3 + 3 + 3 + 3 =$ _____

$9 \times 3 =$ _____

$3 + 3 + 3 + 3 + 3 + 3 + 3 =$ _____

$10 \times 3 =$ _____

$3 + 3 + 3 + 3 =$ _____

$11 \times 3 =$ _____

$3 + 0 =$ _____

$12 \times 3 =$ _____

$3 + 3 + 3 + 3 + 3 + 3 + 3 + 3 + 3 =$ _____

Three Times Table

1. Multiply. Use the key to colour the products.

Colour Key
0 - red
3 - orange
6 - yellow
9 - light green
12 - green
15 - light blue
18 - dark blue
21 - purple
24 - pink
27 - brown
30 - grey
33 - black
36 - gold

$$\begin{array}{r} 0 \\ \times\ 3 \\ \hline \end{array}$$

$$\begin{array}{r} 8 \\ \times\ 3 \\ \hline \end{array}$$

$$\begin{array}{r} 9 \\ \times\ 3 \\ \hline \end{array}$$

$$\begin{array}{r} 3 \\ \times\ 3 \\ \hline \end{array}$$

$$\begin{array}{r} 11 \\ \times\ 3 \\ \hline \end{array}$$

$$\begin{array}{r} 5 \\ \times\ 3 \\ \hline \end{array}$$

$$\begin{array}{r} 7 \\ \times\ 3 \\ \hline \end{array}$$

$$\begin{array}{r} 4 \\ \times\ 3 \\ \hline \end{array}$$

$$\begin{array}{r} 2 \\ \times\ 3 \\ \hline \end{array}$$

$$\begin{array}{r} 6 \\ \times\ 3 \\ \hline \end{array}$$

$$\begin{array}{r} 3 \\ \times\ 3 \\ \hline \end{array}$$

$$\begin{array}{r} 3 \\ \times\ 0 \\ \hline \end{array}$$

$$\begin{array}{r} 3 \\ \times\ 2 \\ \hline \end{array}$$

$$\begin{array}{r} 3 \\ \times\ 9 \\ \hline \end{array}$$

$$\begin{array}{r} 3 \\ \times\ 7 \\ \hline \end{array}$$

$$\begin{array}{r} 3 \\ \times\ 4 \\ \hline \end{array}$$

$$\begin{array}{r} 3 \\ \times\ 6 \\ \hline \end{array}$$

$$\begin{array}{r} 3 \\ \times\ 10 \\ \hline \end{array}$$

$$\begin{array}{r} 1 \\ \times\ 3 \\ \hline \end{array}$$

$$\begin{array}{r} 3 \\ \times\ 8 \\ \hline \end{array}$$

$$\begin{array}{r} 3 \\ \times\ 5 \\ \hline \end{array}$$

$$\begin{array}{r} 3 \\ \times\ 1 \\ \hline \end{array}$$

$$\begin{array}{r} 3 \\ \times\ 12 \\ \hline \end{array}$$

$$\begin{array}{r} 3 \\ \times\ 11 \\ \hline \end{array}$$

Tip for Multiplying by 3
Double the number, and add one more!
For example, 3×5.
Think: $2 \times 5 = 10$. Then add one more 5: $10 + 5 = 15$.
So $3 \times 5 = 15$.

Remember to practice skip counting by 3s!

Three Times Table (continued)

2. Find the product.

> **Watch out! Not all of the letters are used in the answer.**

E	**I**	**G**	**O**	**P**
10 × 3 = ____	7 × 3 = ____	4 × 3 = ____	8 × 3 = ____	2 × 3 = ____
R	**S**	**T**	**V**	**W**
6 × 3 = ____	12 × 3 = ____	9 × 3 = ____	5 × 3 = ____	3 × 3 = ____

Math Riddle: **Why was the broom late?**

___ ___ / ___ ___ ___ ___ ___ ___ ___ ___ ___ !
21 27   24 15 30 18 36 9   30 6   27

3. Find the missing factor.

3 × ___ = 12	___ × 3 = 3	3 × ___ = 6	___ × 3 = 0
___ × 3 = 24	3 × ___ = 27	___ × 3 = 21	3 × ___ = 15
10 × ___ = 30	___ × 3 = 33	3 × ___ = 9	___ × 8 = 24
___ × 3 = 15	3 × ___ = 36	___ × 3 = 30	___ × 3 = 18

1. Find the product. Colour odd products red. Colour even products blue.

9 × 1	1 × 2	9 × 3	4 × 2	4 × 1
3 × 2	5 × 3	1 × 1	7 × 2	6 × 3
5 × 2	2 × 1	0 × 3	2 × 3	3 × 1
0 × 2	5 × 1	2 × 2	6 × 1	8 × 2
3 × 3	9 × 2	7 × 3	6 × 2	8 × 3
0 × 1	4 × 3	7 × 1	1 × 3	8 × 1

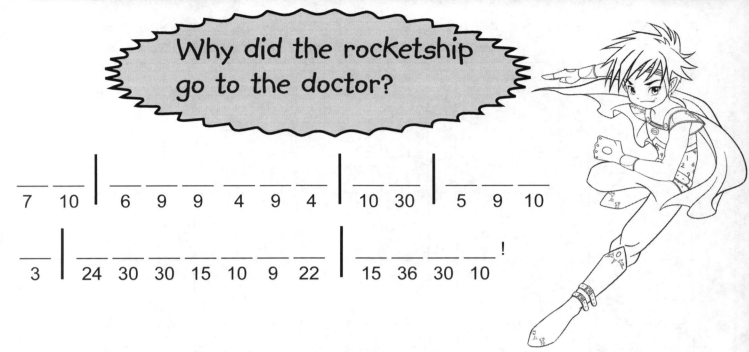

Why did the rocketship go to the doctor?

___ ___ | ___ ___ ___ ___ ___ ___ | ___ ___ | ___ ___ ___
7   10   6   9   9   4   9   4   10   30   5   9   10

___ | ___ ___ ___ ___ ___ ___ ___ | ___ ___ ___ ___ !
3   24 30 30 15 10   9 22   15 36 30 10

A 3 × 1	B 12 × 2	C 8 × 2	D 2 × 2	E 9 × 1
G 5 × 1	H 12 × 3	I 7 × 1	N 3 × 2	O 10 × 3
P 6 × 3	Q 1 × 1	R 11 × 2	S 5 × 3	T 5 × 2

Watch out! Not all of the letters are used in the answer.

Match Multiplication to Addition: Facts for 4

Complete the multiplication facts for 4. Use a multiplication table to help you. Then write the sums. Underline each matching sum and product. Use a different colour for each pair.

$1 \times 4 =$ _____ $4 + 4 + 4 + 4 + 4 =$ _____

$2 \times 4 =$ _____ $4 + 4 + 4 + 4 + 4 + 4 + 4 + 4 + 4 + 4 + 4 + 4 =$ _____

$3 \times 4 =$ _____ $4 + 4 + 4 + 4 + 4 + 4 + 4 =$ _____

$4 \times 4 =$ _____ $4 + 4 + 4 + 4 + 4 + 4 + 4 + 4 + 4 + 4 =$ _____

$5 \times 4 =$ _____ $4 + 4 =$ _____

$6 \times 4 =$ _____ $4 + 0 =$ _____

$7 \times 4 =$ _____ $4 + 4 + 4 + 4 + 4 + 4 =$ _____

$8 \times 4 =$ _____ $4 + 4 + 4 + 4 + 4 + 4 + 4 + 4 + 4 + 4 + 4 =$ _____

$9 \times 4 =$ _____ $4 + 4 + 4 + 4 + 4 =$ _____

$10 \times 4 =$ _____ $4 + 4 + 4 + 4 + 4 + 4 + 4 + 4 =$ _____

$11 \times 4 =$ _____ $4 + 4 + 4 + 4 + 4 + 4 + 4 + 4 + 4 =$ _____

$12 \times 4 =$ _____ $4 + 4 + 4 =$ _____

Four Times Table

1. Multiply. Use the key to colour the products.

Colour Key
0 - red
4 - orange
8 - yellow
12 - light green
16 - green
20 - light blue
24 - dark blue
28 - purple
32 - pink
36 - brown
40 - grey
44 - black
48 - gold

9 × 4	0 × 4	7 × 4	8 × 4	6 × 4
3 × 4	2 × 4	4 × 4	5 × 4	12 × 4
1 × 4	4 × 2	4 × 8	4 × 9	4 × 7	11 × 4
4 × 12	4 × 6	4 × 10	4 × 5	4 × 1	4 × 3

4
× 11

4
× 0

Tip for Multiplying by 4
$2 \times 2 = 4$, so double the number, then double the answer you get.
For example, 5×4.
Think: $5 \times 2 = 10$. Then $10 \times 2 = 20$. So $5 \times 4 = 20$.

Remember to practice skip counting by 4s!

Four Times Table (continued)

Watch out! Not all of the letters are used in the answer.

2. Find the product.

A	B	C	E	G
0 × 4 = ____	3 × 4 = ____	8 × 4 = ____	2 × 4 = ____	12 × 4 = ____

L	U	K	R	T
9 × 4 = ____	5 × 4 = ____	11 × 4 = ____	6 × 4 = ____	7 × 4 = ____

Math Riddle: **What vehicle has four wheels and flies?**

___ / ___ ___ ___ ___ ___ ___ ___ / ___ ___ ___ ___ ___
0   48   0   24   12   0   48   8   28   24   20   32   44

3. Find the missing factor.

3 × ___ = 12	___ × 4 = 8	4 × ___ = 24	___ × 4 = 32
___ × 4 = 16	4 × ___ = 28	___ × 4 = 36	4 × ___ = 44
10 × ___ = 40	___ × 4 = 8	4 × ___ = 48	___ × 4 = 24
___ × 9 = 36	4 × ___ = 20	___ × 4 = 4	___ × 4 = 0

Complete the multiplication facts for 5. Use a multiplication table to help you. Then write the sums. Underline each matching sum and product. Use a different colour for each pair.

$1 \times 5 = $ _____

$5 + 5 + 5 + 5 = $ _____

$2 \times 5 = $ _____

$5 + 5 + 5 + 5 + 5 = $ _____

$3 \times 5 = $ _____

$5 + 5 + 5 + 5 + 5 + 5 + 5 + 5 + 5 + 5 + 5 = $ _____

$4 \times 5 = $ _____

$5 + 5 + 5 + 5 + 5 + 5 + 5 + 5 + 5 = $ _____

$5 \times 5 = $ _____

$5 + 5 + 5 + 5 + 5 + 5 + 5 + 5 + 5 + 5 + 5 + 5 = $ _____

$6 \times 5 = $ _____

$5 + 0 = $ _____

$7 \times 5 = $ _____

$5 + 5 + 5 + 5 + 5 + 5 + 5 + 5 + 5 + 5 = $ _____

$8 \times 5 = $ _____

$5 + 5 + 5 = $ _____

$9 \times 5 = $ _____

$5 + 5 = $ _____

$10 \times 5 = $ _____

$5 + 5 + 5 + 5 + 5 + 5 = $ _____

$11 \times 5 = $ _____

$5 + 5 + 5 + 5 + 5 + 5 + 5 = $ _____

$12 \times 5 = $ _____

$5 + 5 + 5 + 5 + 5 + 5 + 5 + 5 = $ _____

Five Times Table

1. Multiply. Use the key to colour the products.

Colour Key
0 - red
5 - orange
10 - yellow
15 - light green
20 - green
25 - light blue
30 - dark blue
35 - purple
40 - pink
45 - brown
50 - grey
55 - black
60 - gold

6 × 5	0 × 5	7 × 5	9 × 5	8 × 5
1 × 5	2 × 5	11 × 5	3 × 5	4 × 5
5 × 5	12 × 5	5 × 2	5 × 0	5 × 9	5 × 4
5 × 11	5 × 6	5 × 3	5 × 8	5 × 1	5 × 12
5 × 10	5 × 7				

Tip for Multiplying by 5
The answer always ends in 5 or 0.
The product is half the number times 10.
For example, for 5 x 6, half of 6 is 3.
10 × 3 = 30. So 5 × 6 = 30.

Remember to practice skip counting by 5s!

Five Times Table (continued)

2. Find the product.

Watch out! Not all of the letters are used in the answer.

A	E	F	H	L
$7 \times 5 =$ ___	$9 \times 5 =$ ___	$1 \times 5 =$ ___	$4 \times 5 =$ ___	$12 \times 5 =$ ___

M	O	P	S	T
$6 \times 5 =$ ___	$3 \times 5 =$ ___	$8 \times 5 =$ ___	$10 \times 5 =$ ___	$5 \times 5 =$ ___

Math Riddle: **How many months of the year have 28 days?**

___ ___ ___ / ___ ___ / ___ ___ ___ ___ !
35 60 60   15   5   25 20 45 30

3. Find the missing factor.

$3 \times$ __ $= 15$	__ $\times 5 = 20$	$5 \times$ __ $= 55$	__ $\times 5 = 10$
__ $\times 5 = 45$	__ $\times 5 = 0$	__ $\times 5 = 40$	$5 \times$ __ $= 30$
$1 \times$ __ $= 5$	__ $\times 5 = 35$	$5 \times$ __ $= 5$	__ $\times 5 = 25$
__ $\times 5 = 15$	$2 \times$ __ $= 10$	__ $\times 12 = 60$	$10 \times$ __ $= 50$

Complete the multiplication facts for 6. Use a multiplication table to help you. Then write the sums. Underline each matching sum and product. Use a different colour for each pair.

$1 \times 6 =$ _____

$6 + 6 + 6 + 6 + 6 + 6 =$ _____

$2 \times 6 =$ _____

$6 + 6 + 6 + 6 + 6 + 6 + 6 + 6 + 6 + 6 + 6 =$ _____

$3 \times 6 =$ _____

$6 + 6 + 6 + 6 + 6 + 6 + 6 + 6 + 6 =$ _____

$4 \times 6 =$ _____

$6 + 6 + 6 + 6 + 6 + 6 + 6 =$ _____

$5 \times 6 =$ _____

$6 + 6 =$ _____

$6 \times 6 =$ _____

$6 + 6 + 6 + 6 + 6 + 6 + 6 + 6 + 6 + 6 + 6 + 6 =$ _____

$7 \times 6 =$ _____

$6 + 6 + 6 + 6 =$ _____

$8 \times 6 =$ _____

$6 + 0 =$ _____

$9 \times 6 =$ _____

$6 + 6 + 6 =$ _____

$10 \times 6 =$ _____

$6 + 6 + 6 + 6 + 6 + 6 + 6 + 6 =$ _____

$11 \times 6 =$ _____

$6 + 6 + 6 + 6 + 6 =$ _____

$12 \times 6 =$ _____

$6 + 6 + 6 + 6 + 6 + 6 + 6 + 6 + 6 + 6 =$ _____

1. Multiply. Use the key to colour the products.

Colour Key
0 - red
6 - orange
12 - yellow
18 - light green
24 - green
30 - light blue
36 - dark blue
42 - purple
48 - pink
54 - brown
60 - grey
66 - black
72 - gold

$$2 \times 6$$

$$0 \times 6$$

$$9 \times 6$$

$$3 \times 6$$

$$1 \times 6$$

$$7 \times 6$$

$$8 \times 6$$

$$4 \times 6$$

$$5 \times 6$$

$$6 \times 6$$

$$6 \times 12$$

$$11 \times 6$$

$$6 \times 2$$

$$6 \times 0$$

$$6 \times 9$$

$$6 \times 4$$

$$6 \times 10$$

$$6 \times 7$$

$$6 \times 1$$

$$6 \times 5$$

$$12 \times 6$$

$$6 \times 3$$

$$6 \times 11$$

$$6 \times 8$$

Tip for Multiplying by 6
When multiplying 6 by an even number, the answer always ends in the same number you multiplied 6 by. For example, 6 × **2** = 1**2**.
In the answer, the tens column is always half the ones column. For example, 6 × **6** = **3**6.

Remember to practice skip counting by 6s!

Six Times Table (continued)

2. Find the product.

A	B	E	H	I
3 × 6 = ____	11 × 6 = ____	8 × 6 = ____	9 × 6 = ____	5 × 6 = ____

K	N	R	T	V
2 × 6 = ____	10 × 6 = ____	6 × 6 = ____	12 × 6 = ____	4 × 6 = ____

Math Riddle: **Where do some fish keep their money?**

___ ___ ___ / ___ ___ ___ ___ ___ / ___ ___ ___ ___ !
72 54 48   36 30 24 48 36   66 18 60 12

3. Find the missing factor.

6 × ___ = 66	___ × 6 = 24	6 × ___ = 36	___ × 6 = 48
___ × 6 = 42	10 × ___ = 60	___ × 6 = 0	6 × ___ = 18
1 × ___ = 6	___ × 8 = 48	6 × ___ = 54	___ × 6 = 12
___ × 6 = 30	6 × ___ = 6	___ × 6 = 18	___ × 6 = 72

Multiply by 4, 5, and 6

1. Find the product. Colour odd products red. Colour even products blue.

9 × 4	11 × 6	9 × 5	4 × 6	4 × 4
3 × 6	3 × 5	11 × 4	7 × 6	3 × 6
5 × 6	2 × 4	12 × 5	10 × 5	3 × 4
12 × 6	5 × 4	2 × 6	6 × 4	8 × 6
3 × 5	9 × 6	7 × 5	6 × 6	8 × 5
12 × 4	4 × 5	7 × 4	11 × 5	8 × 4

Math Riddle: Multiplication Facts for 4, 5, and 6

Where do aliens go to school?

$\overline{}\ \overline{}$ | $\overline{}$ | $\overline{}\ \overline{}\ \overline{}\ \overline{}\ \overline{}\ \overline{}\ \overline{}\ \overline{}$ **-** $\overline{}\ \overline{}\ \overline{}$!
28 54 | 28 | 24 36 40 60 6 32 20 6   40 54 30

A $\begin{array}{r} 7 \\ \times\,4 \\ \hline \end{array}$	C $\begin{array}{r} 3 \\ \times\,5 \\ \hline \end{array}$	E $\begin{array}{r} 1 \\ \times\,6 \\ \hline \end{array}$	I $\begin{array}{r} 10 \\ \times\,4 \\ \hline \end{array}$	L $\begin{array}{r} 9 \\ \times\,5 \\ \hline \end{array}$
M $\begin{array}{r} 11 \\ \times\,6 \\ \hline \end{array}$	N $\begin{array}{r} 9 \\ \times\,4 \\ \hline \end{array}$	O $\begin{array}{r} 5 \\ \times\,5 \\ \hline \end{array}$	P $\begin{array}{r} 2 \\ \times\,6 \\ \hline \end{array}$	R $\begin{array}{r} 8 \\ \times\,4 \\ \hline \end{array}$
S $\begin{array}{r} 4 \\ \times\,5 \\ \hline \end{array}$	T $\begin{array}{r} 9 \\ \times\,6 \\ \hline \end{array}$	U $\begin{array}{r} 6 \\ \times\,4 \\ \hline \end{array}$	V $\begin{array}{r} 12 \\ \times\,5 \\ \hline \end{array}$	Y $\begin{array}{r} 5 \\ \times\,6 \\ \hline \end{array}$

Watch out! Not all of the letters are used in the answer.

Match Multiplication to Addition: Facts for 7

Complete the multiplication facts for 7. Use a multiplication table to help you. Then write the sums. Underline each matching sum and product. Use a different colour for each pair.

1 × 7 = _____   7 + 7 + 7 + 7 + 7 + 7 + 7 + 7 + 7 + 7 + 7 + 7 = _____

2 × 7 = _____   7 + 7 + 7 + 7 + 7 + 7 + 7 + 7 + 7 = _____

3 × 7 = _____   7 + 7 + 7 + 7 + 7 = _____

4 × 7 = _____   7 + 7 + 7 + 7 + 7 + 7 = _____

5 × 7 = _____   7 + 7 = _____

6 × 7 = _____   7 + 7 + 7 + 7 + 7 + 7 + 7 + 7 + 7 + 7 = _____

7 × 7 = _____   7 + 7 + 7 + 7 = _____

8 × 7 = _____   7 + 7 + 7 + 7 + 7 + 7 + 7 + 7 + 7 + 7 + 7 = _____

9 × 7 = _____   7 + 7 + 7 = _____

10 × 7 = _____   7 + 7 + 7 + 7 + 7 + 7 + 7 = _____

11 × 7 = _____   7 + 0 = _____

12 × 7 = _____   7 + 7 + 7 + 7 + 7 + 7 + 7 + 7 = _____

Seven Times Table

1. Multiply. Use the key to colour the products.

Colour Key
0 - red
14 - yellow
21 - light green
28 - green
35 - light blue
42 - dark blue
49 - purple
56 - pink
63 - brown
70 - grey
77 - black
84 - gold

$$\begin{array}{r} 3 \\ \times\ 7 \\ \hline \end{array}$$

$$\begin{array}{r} 0 \\ \times\ 7 \\ \hline \end{array}$$

$$\begin{array}{r} 8 \\ \times\ 7 \\ \hline \end{array}$$

$$\begin{array}{r} 6 \\ \times\ 7 \\ \hline \end{array}$$

$$\begin{array}{r} 11 \\ \times\ 7 \\ \hline \end{array}$$

$$\begin{array}{r} 12 \\ 7 \\ \hline \end{array}$$

$$\begin{array}{r} 7 \\ \times\ 7 \\ \hline \end{array}$$

$$\begin{array}{r} 4 \\ \times\ 7 \\ \hline \end{array}$$

$$\begin{array}{r} 2 \\ \times\ 7 \\ \hline \end{array}$$

$$\begin{array}{r} 9 \\ \times\ 7 \\ \hline \end{array}$$

$$\begin{array}{r} 5 \\ \times\ 7 \\ \hline \end{array}$$

$$\begin{array}{r} 7 \\ \times\ 2 \\ \hline \end{array}$$

$$\begin{array}{r} 7 \\ \times\ 8 \\ \hline \end{array}$$

$$\begin{array}{r} 1 \\ \times\ 7 \\ \hline \end{array}$$

$$\begin{array}{r} 7 \\ \times\ 12 \\ \hline \end{array}$$

$$\begin{array}{r} 7 \\ \times\ 4 \\ \hline \end{array}$$

$$\begin{array}{r} 7 \\ \times\ 11 \\ \hline \end{array}$$

$$\begin{array}{r} 7 \\ \times\ 5 \\ \hline \end{array}$$

$$\begin{array}{r} 7 \\ \times\ 3 \\ \hline \end{array}$$

$$\begin{array}{r} 7 \\ \times\ 6 \\ \hline \end{array}$$

$$\begin{array}{r} 7 \\ \times\ 9 \\ \hline \end{array}$$

$$\begin{array}{r} 7 \\ \times\ 1 \\ \hline \end{array}$$

$$\begin{array}{r} 7 \\ \times\ 0 \\ \hline \end{array}$$

$$\begin{array}{r} 7 \\ \times\ 10 \\ \hline \end{array}$$

Tip for Multiplying by 7
Multiply 7 by a number that you know close to the number.
For 7 × 7 =, you know 5 × 7 = 35. Then 7 – 5 = 2 more 7s.
Multiply the remaining 7s and add them to your answer.
Think: 5 × 7 = 35, and 2 × 7 = 14.
35 + 14 = 49. So 7 × 7 = 49.

Remember to practice skip counting by 7s!

Seven Times Table (continued)

2. Find the product.

| | Watch out! Not all of the letters are used in the answer. |

A 5 × 7 = ____	**C** 7 × 7 = ____	**D** 3 × 7 = ____	**E** 10 × 7 = ____	**H** 8 × 7 = ____
L 12 × 7 = ____	**M** 4 × 7 = ____	**O** 6 × 7 = ____	**P** 9 × 7 = ____	**S** 11 × 7 = ____

Math Riddle: **What kind of dog loves to have baths?**

___ / ___ ___ ___ ___ ___ ___ ___ ___ ___ ___ !
35   77 56 35 28 63 42 42 21 84 70

3. Find the missing factor.

2 × ___ = 14	___ × 7 = 7	3 × ___ = 21	___ × 7 = 56
___ × 7 = 70	12 × ___ = 84	___ × 6 = 42	7 × ___ = 49
7 × ___ = 56	___ × 7 = 35	7 × ___ = 70	___ × 7 = 0
___ × 7 = 77	7 × ___ = 14	___ × 7 = 63	___ × 7 = 28

Match Multiplication to Addition: Facts for 8

Complete the multiplication facts for 8. Use a multiplication table to help you. Then write the sums. Underline each matching sum and product. Use a different colour for each pair.

1 × 8 = _____   8 + 8 + 8 + 8 + 8 + 8 + 8 + 8 + 8 + 8 + 8 = _____

2 × 8 = _____   8 + 8 + 8 + 8 + 8 + 8 = _____

3 × 8 = _____   8 + 8 + 8 + 8 + 8 + 8 + 8 + 8 + 8 + 8 = _____

4 × 8 = _____   8 + 8 = _____

5 × 8 = _____   8 + 8 + 8 + 8 + 8 + 8 + 8 + 8 + 8 + 8 + 8 + 8 = _____

6 × 8 = _____   8 + 8 + 8 + 8 + 8 + 8 + 8 + 8 = _____

7 × 8 = _____   8 + 8 + 8 = _____

8 × 8 = _____   8 + 8 + 8 + 8 + 8 = _____

9 × 8 = _____   8 + 0 = _____

10 × 8 = _____   8 + 8 + 8 + 8 = _____

11 × 8 = _____   8 + 8 + 8 + 8 + 8 + 8 + 8 = _____

12 × 8 = _____   8 + 8 + 8 + 8 + 8 + 8 + 8 + 8 + 8 = _____

Eight Times Table

1. Multiply. Use the key to colour the products.

Colour Key
0 - red
8 - orange
16 - yellow
24 - light green
32 - green
40 - light blue
48 - dark blue
56 - purple
64 - pink
72 - brown
80 - grey
88 - black
96 - gold

$$\begin{array}{r} 3 \\ \times\ 8 \\ \hline \end{array}$$

$$\begin{array}{r} 9 \\ \times\ 8 \\ \hline \end{array}$$

$$\begin{array}{r} 8 \\ \times\ 8 \\ \hline \end{array}$$

$$\begin{array}{r} 0 \\ \times\ 8 \\ \hline \end{array}$$

$$\begin{array}{r} 11 \\ \times\ 8 \\ \hline \end{array}$$

$$\begin{array}{r} 5 \\ \times\ 8 \\ \hline \end{array}$$

$$\begin{array}{r} 7 \\ \times\ 8 \\ \hline \end{array}$$

$$\begin{array}{r} 4 \\ \times\ 8 \\ \hline \end{array}$$

$$\begin{array}{r} 2 \\ \times\ 8 \\ \hline \end{array}$$

$$\begin{array}{r} 6 \\ \times\ 8 \\ \hline \end{array}$$

$$\begin{array}{r} 1 \\ \times\ 8 \\ \hline \end{array}$$

$$\begin{array}{r} 12 \\ \times\ 8 \\ \hline \end{array}$$

$$\begin{array}{r} 8 \\ \times\ 2 \\ \hline \end{array}$$

$$\begin{array}{r} 8 \\ \times\ 5 \\ \hline \end{array}$$

$$\begin{array}{r} 8 \\ \times\ 9 \\ \hline \end{array}$$

$$\begin{array}{r} 8 \\ \times\ 4 \\ \hline \end{array}$$

$$\begin{array}{r} 8 \\ \times\ 11 \\ \hline \end{array}$$

$$\begin{array}{r} 8 \\ \times\ 6 \\ \hline \end{array}$$

$$\begin{array}{r} 8 \\ \times\ 3 \\ \hline \end{array}$$

$$\begin{array}{r} 8 \\ \times\ 7 \\ \hline \end{array}$$

$$\begin{array}{r} 8 \\ \times\ 12 \\ \hline \end{array}$$

$$\begin{array}{r} 8 \\ \times\ 1 \\ \hline \end{array}$$

$$\begin{array}{r} 8 \\ \times\ 10 \\ \hline \end{array}$$

$$\begin{array}{r} 8 \\ \times\ 0 \\ \hline \end{array}$$

Tip for Multiplying by 8
Doubling 4 gives you 8, so double the number you multiply by 4 to get the multiple for 8!
For 8 × 8 =, you know that 4 × 8 = 32.
Next, double the 32: 32 × 2 = 64. So 8 × 8 = 64.

Remember to practice skip counting by 8s!

Eight Times Table (continued)

2. Find the product.

Watch out! Not all of the letters are used in the answer.

A	**C**	**E**	**H**	**M**
8 × 8 = ____	2 × 8 = ____	12 × 8 = ____	9 × 8 = ____	0 × 8 = ____

P	**R**	**S**	**T**	**W**
4 × 8 = ____	10 × 8 = ____	5 × 8 = ____	6 × 8 = ____	7 × 8 = ____

Math Riddle: **What do cats like to read in the morning?**

___ ___ ___ / ___ ___ ___ ___ ___ ___ ___ ___ ___ !
48 72 96   0   96 56 40 32 64 32 96 80

3. Find the missing factor.

4 × ___ = 32	___ × 8 = 56	2 × ___ = 16	___ × 8 = 96
___ × 8 = 40	8 × ___ = 32	___ × 8 = 8	10 × ___ = 80
12 × ___ = 96	___ × 8 = 24	8 × ___ = 72	___ × 8 = 88
___ × 8 = 48	3 × ___ = 24	___ × 8 = 64	___ × 8 = 0

Match Multiplication to Addition: Facts for 9

Complete the multiplication facts for 9. Use a multiplication table to help you. Then write the sums. Underline each matching sum and product. Use a different colour for each pair.

1 × 9 = _____   9 + 9 + 9 + 9 + 9 + 9 + 9 + 9 + 9 + 9 + 9 + 9 = _____

2 × 9 = _____   9 + 9 + 9 + 9 + 9 + 9 + 9 = _____

3 × 9 = _____   9 + 9 + 9 + 9 + 9 + 9 + 9 + 9 + 9 + 9 + 9 = _____

4 × 9 = _____   9 + 9 + 9 + 9 + 9 + 9 = _____

5 × 9 = _____   9 + 0 = _____

6 × 9 = _____   9 + 9 + 9 + 9 = _____

7 × 9 = _____   9 + 9 = _____

8 × 9 = _____   9 + 9 + 9 + 9 + 9 + 9 + 9 + 9 + 9 + 9 = _____

9 × 9 = _____   9 + 9 + 9 + 9 + 9 + 9 + 9 + 9 + 9 = _____

10 × 9 = _____   9 + 9 + 9 + 9 + 9 + 9 + 9 + 9 = _____

11 × 9 = _____   9 + 9 + 9 + 9 + 9 = _____

12 × 9 = _____   9 + 9 + 9 = _____

Nine Times Table

1. Multiply. Use the key to colour the products.

Colour Key
0 - red
9 - orange
18 - yellow
27 - light green
36 - green
45 - light blue
54 - dark blue
63 - purple
72 - pink
81 - brown
90 - grey
99 - black
108 - gold

$$\begin{array}{r} 7 \\ \times\ 9 \\ \hline \end{array}$$

$$\begin{array}{r} 6 \\ \times\ 9 \\ \hline \end{array}$$

$$\begin{array}{r} 3 \\ \times\ 9 \\ \hline \end{array}$$

$$\begin{array}{r} 1 \\ \times\ 9 \\ \hline \end{array}$$

$$\begin{array}{r} 0 \\ \times\ 9 \\ \hline \end{array}$$

$$\begin{array}{r} 5 \\ \times\ 9 \\ \hline \end{array}$$

$$\begin{array}{r} 2 \\ \times\ 9 \\ \hline \end{array}$$

$$\begin{array}{r} 4 \\ \times\ 9 \\ \hline \end{array}$$

$$\begin{array}{r} 8 \\ \times\ 9 \\ \hline \end{array}$$

$$\begin{array}{r} 12 \\ \times\ 9 \\ \hline \end{array}$$

$$\begin{array}{r} 9 \\ \times\ 9 \\ \hline \end{array}$$

$$\begin{array}{r} 9 \\ \times\ 6 \\ \hline \end{array}$$

$$\begin{array}{r} 9 \\ \times\ 2 \\ \hline \end{array}$$

$$\begin{array}{r} 9 \\ \times\ 7 \\ \hline \end{array}$$

$$\begin{array}{r} 11 \\ \times\ 9 \\ \hline \end{array}$$

$$\begin{array}{r} 9 \\ \times\ 4 \\ \hline \end{array}$$

$$\begin{array}{r} 9 \\ \times\ 1 \\ \hline \end{array}$$

$$\begin{array}{r} 9 \\ \times\ 8 \\ \hline \end{array}$$

$$\begin{array}{r} 9 \\ \times\ 3 \\ \hline \end{array}$$

$$\begin{array}{r} 9 \\ \times\ 5 \\ \hline \end{array}$$

$$\begin{array}{r} 9 \\ \times\ 12 \\ \hline \end{array}$$

$$\begin{array}{r} 9 \\ \times\ 10 \\ \hline \end{array}$$

$$\begin{array}{r} 9 \\ \times\ 0 \\ \hline \end{array}$$

$$\begin{array}{r} 9 \\ \times\ 11 \\ \hline \end{array}$$

Tip for Multiplying by 9
Multiply the number by 10, then subtract one of that number from the answer. For example,
7 × 9 =
Think: 7 × 10 = 70. 70 − 7 = 63. So 7 × 9 = 63.

Remember to practice skip counting by 9s!

2. Find the product.

A 12 × 9 = ____	**E** 6 × 9 = ____	**G** 11 × 9 = ____	**I** 8 × 9 = ____	**L** 0 × 9 = ____
N 10 × 9 = ____	**P** 1 × 9 = ____	**S** 7 × 9 = ____	**T** 5 × 9 = ____	**W** 4 × 9 = ____

Math Riddle: **Why did the banana go to the doctor?**

___ ___ / ___ ___ ___ ___ ___ / ___ ___ ___ ___ ___ ___ ___ /
72 45   36 108 63 90 45   9 54 54 0 72 90 99

___ ___ ___ ___ !
36 54 0   0

3. Find the missing factor.

9 × __ = 18	9 × __ = 45	11 × __ = 99	__ × 9 = 81
__ × 9 = 0	__ × 9 = 36	__ × 9 = 54	9 × __ = 27
10 × __ = 90	__ × 9 = 108	9 × __ = 9	__ × 9 = 45
9 × __ = 99	__ × 9 = 72	__ × 9 = 63	2 × __ = 18

Multiply by 7, 8, and 9

1. Find the product. Colour odd products red. Colour even products blue.

9 × 7	11 × 9	9 × 8	4 × 9	4 × 7
3 × 9	5 × 8	11 × 7	7 × 9	6 × 8
5 × 9	2 × 7	12 × 8	10 × 8	3 × 7
12 × 9	5 × 7	2 × 9	6 × 7	8 × 9
3 × 8	9 × 9	7 × 8	6 × 9	8 × 8
12 × 7	4 × 8	7 × 7	11 × 8	10 × 7

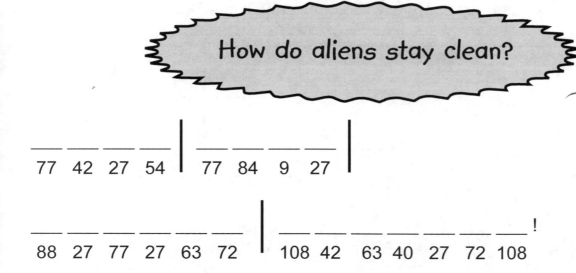

How do aliens stay clean?

___ ___ ___ ___ | ___ ___ ___ ___ |
77 42 27 54   77 84 9   27

___ ___ ___ ___ ___ ___ | ___ ___ ___ ___ ___ ___ ___ !
88 27 77 27 63 72   108 42 63 40 27 72 108

A 12 ×7	D 8 ×8	E 3 ×9	H 6 ×7	I 2 ×8
K 1 ×9	L 3 ×7	M 11 ×8	O 7 ×9	P 10 ×7
R 9 ×8	S 12 ×9	T 11 ×7	W 5 ×8	Y 6 ×9

Watch out! Not all of the letters are used in the answer.

Match Multiplication to Addition: Facts for 10

Complete the multiplication facts for 10. Use a multiplication table to help you. Then write the sums. Underline each matching sum and product. Use a different colour for each pair.

$1 \times 10 =$ _____ $10 + 10 + 10 + 10 + 10 =$ _____

$2 \times 10 =$ _____ $10 + 10 + 10 + 10 =$ _____

$3 \times 10 =$ _____ $10 + 10 + 10 + 10 + 10 + 10 + 10 + 10 =$ _____

$4 \times 10 =$ _____ $10 + 10 + 10 + 10 + 10 + 10 + 10 =$ _____

$5 \times 10 =$ _____ $10 + 10 + 10 + 10 + 10 + 10 + 10 + 10 + 10 + 10 =$ _____

$6 \times 10 =$ _____ $10 + 10 + 10 =$ _____

$7 \times 10 =$ _____ $10 + 0 =$ _____

$8 \times 10 =$ _____ $10 + 10 + 10 + 10 + 10 + 10 + 10 + 10 + 10 =$ _____

$9 \times 10 =$ _____ $10 + 10 + 10 + 10 + 10 + 10 + 10 + 10 + 10 + 10 + 10 + 10 =$ _____

$10 \times 10 =$ _____ $10 + 10 + 10 + 10 + 10 + 10 + 10 + 10 + 10 + 10 + 10 =$ _____

$11 \times 10 =$ _____ $10 + 10 =$ _____

$12 \times 10 =$ _____ $10 + 10 + 10 + 10 + 10 + 10 =$ _____

Ten Times Table

1. Multiply. Use the key to colour the products.

Colour Key
0 - red
10 - orange
20 - yellow
30 - light green
40 - green
50 - light blue
60 - dark blue
70 - purple
80 - pink
90 - brown
100 - grey
110 - black
120 - gold

$$9 \times 10$$

$$6 \times 10$$

$$3 \times 10$$

$$8 \times 10$$

$$0 \times 10$$

$$4 \times 10$$

$$2 \times 10$$

$$5 \times 10$$

$$7 \times 10$$

$$11 \times 10$$

$$10 \times 3$$

$$10 \times 8$$

$$10 \times 10$$

$$10 \times 6$$

$$10 \times 9$$

$$10 \times 1$$

$$10 \times 11$$

$$10 \times 2$$

$$10 \times 7$$

$$10 \times 5$$

$$10 \times 12$$

$$10 \times 4$$

$$10 \times 10$$

$$10 \times 0$$

Tip for Multiplying by 10
When multiplying by 10, just add 0!
For example, 6 × 10 = 60.

Remember to practice skip counting by 10s!

© Chalkboard Publishing

2. Find the product.

E	F	G	H	I
12 × 10 = ____	4 × 10 = ____	5 × 10 = ____	10 × 10 = ____	0 × 10 = ____

K	R	O	T	Y
11 × 10 = ____	1 × 10 = ____	6 × 10 = ____	9 × 10 = ____	3 × 10 = ____

Math Riddle: **Why was the piano locked out?**

___ ___ / ___ ___ ___ ___ ___ ___ / ___ ___ ___ / ___ ___ ___ !
 0   90   40   60   10   50   60   90   90 100 120   110 120   30

3. Find the missing factor.

2 × ____ = 20	____ × 10 = 60	10 × ____ = 110	____ × 10 = 50
____ × 2 = 20	10 × ____ = 70	____ × 10 = 0	10 × ____ = 10
10 × ____ = 90	____ × 10 = 80	5 × ____ = 50	____ × 10 = 100
____ × 10 = 40	10 × ____ = 110	____ × 12 = 120	3 × ___ = 30

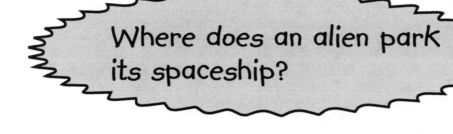

Where does an alien park its spaceship?

$$\overline{40}\ \overline{96}\ \Big|\ \overline{40}\ \Big|\ \overline{48}\ \overline{40}\ \overline{18}\ \overline{25}\ \overline{44}\ \overline{14}\ \overline{3}\ \Big|$$

$$\overline{24}\ \overline{63}\ \overline{96}\ \overline{63}\ \overline{120}\ \overline{18}\ !$$

A	C	E	G	I	K
10 × 4	3 × 5	7 × 9	1 × 3	11 × 4	5 × 5

L	M	N	O	P	R
8 × 1	4 × 6	2 × 7	12 × 10	6 × 8	9 × 2

S	T
5 × 10	12 × 8

Watch out! Not all of the letters are used in the answer.

Match Multiplication to Addition: Facts for 11

Complete the multiplication facts for 11. Use a multiplication table to help you. Then write the sums. Underline each matching sum and product. Use a different colour for each pair.

1 × 11 = _____   11 + 11 + 11 + 11 + 11 + 11 + 11 + 11 + 11 = _____

2 × 11 = _____   11 + 11 + 11 + 11 + 11 + 11 + 11 = _____

3 × 11 = _____   11 + 11 + 11 + 11 + 11 + 11 + 11 + 11 + 11 + 11 + 11 + 11 = _____

4 × 11 = _____   11 + 11 + 11 + 11 + 11 + 11 + 11 + 11 + 11 + 11 + 11 = _____

5 × 11 = _____   11 + 11 + 11 + 11 + 11 = _____

6 × 11 = _____   11 + 11 + 11 + 11 + 11 + 11 + 11 + 11 = _____

7 × 11 = _____   11 + 11 + 11 + 11 + 11 + 11 + 11 + 11 + 11 + 11 = _____

8 × 11 = _____   11 + 11 + 11 = _____

9 × 11 = _____   11 + 0 = _____

10 × 11 = _____   11 + 11 + 11 + 11 = _____

11 × 11 = _____   11 + 11 + 11 + 11 + 11 + 11 = _____

12 × 11 = _____   11 + 11 = _____

Eleven Times Table

1. Multiply. Use the key to colour the products.

Colour Key
0 - red
11 - orange
22 - yellow
33 - light green
44 - green
55 - light blue
66 - dark blue
77 - purple
88 - pink
99 - brown
110 - grey
121 - black
132 - gold

0 × 11	

$$\begin{array}{r} 0 \\ \times\ 11 \\ \hline \end{array} \qquad \begin{array}{r} 8 \\ \times\ 11 \\ \hline \end{array} \qquad \begin{array}{r} 3 \\ \times\ 11 \\ \hline \end{array} \qquad \begin{array}{r} 9 \\ \times\ 11 \\ \hline \end{array} \qquad \begin{array}{r} 6 \\ \times\ 11 \\ \hline \end{array}$$

$$\begin{array}{r} 2 \\ \times\ 11 \\ \hline \end{array} \qquad \begin{array}{r} 4 \\ \times\ 11 \\ \hline \end{array} \qquad \begin{array}{r} 5 \\ \times\ 11 \\ \hline \end{array} \qquad \begin{array}{r} 7 \\ \times\ 11 \\ \hline \end{array} \qquad \begin{array}{r} 1 \\ \times\ 11 \\ \hline \end{array}$$

$$\begin{array}{r} 11 \\ \times\ 8 \\ \hline \end{array} \qquad \begin{array}{r} 12 \\ \times\ 11 \\ \hline \end{array} \qquad \begin{array}{r} 11 \\ \times\ 2 \\ \hline \end{array} \qquad \begin{array}{r} 11 \\ \times\ 7 \\ \hline \end{array} \qquad \begin{array}{r} 11 \\ \times\ 9 \\ \hline \end{array} \qquad \begin{array}{r} 11 \\ \times\ 4 \\ \hline \end{array}$$

$$\begin{array}{r} 11 \\ \times\ 11 \\ \hline \end{array} \qquad \begin{array}{r} 11 \\ \times\ 6 \\ \hline \end{array} \qquad \begin{array}{r} 11 \\ \times\ 5 \\ \hline \end{array} \qquad \begin{array}{r} 11 \\ \times\ 3 \\ \hline \end{array} \qquad \begin{array}{r} 11 \\ \times\ 12 \\ \hline \end{array} \qquad \begin{array}{r} 11 \\ \times\ 0 \\ \hline \end{array}$$

$$\begin{array}{r} 11 \\ \times\ 10 \\ \hline \end{array} \qquad \begin{array}{r} 11 \\ \times\ 1 \\ \hline \end{array}$$

Tip for Multiplying by 11
When multiplying a number up to 9 × 11, just write the digit twice!
For example, 5 × 11 = 55.

Remember to practice skip counting by 11s!

Eleven Times Table (continued)

2. Find the product.

Watch out! Not all of the letters are used in the answer.

A	**E**	**I**	**L**	**M**
11 × 11 = ____	7 × 11 = ____	0 × 11 = ____	9 × 11 = ____	4 × 11 = ____

P	**Q**	**S**	**T**	**U**
12 × 11 = ____	8 × 11 = ____	5 × 11 = ____	3 × 11 = ____	6 × 11 = ____

Math Riddle: **What vegetables do librarians like the most?**

___ ___ ___ ___ ___ / ___ ___ ___ ___ !
88 66 0 77 33   132 77 121 55

3. Find the missing factor.

11 × ____ = 33	____ × 11 = 66	5 × ____ = 55	____ × 11 = 44
____ × 6 = 66	11 × ____ = 121	____ × 1 = 11	11 × ____ = 77
10 × ____ = 110	____ × 2 = 22	11 × ____ = 88	____ × 11 = 55
____ × 11 = 132	11 × ____ = 11	____ × 11 = 99	__ × 11 = 0

Match Multiplication to Addition: Facts for 12

Complete the multiplication facts for 12. Use a multiplication table to help you. Then write the sums. Underline each matching sum and product. Use a different colour for each pair.

1 × 12 = ___   12 + 12 + 12 + 12 + 12 + 12 + 12 + 12 = ____

2 × 12 = ____   12 + 12 + 12 + 12 + 12 + 12 + 12 = _____

3 × 12 = ____   12 + 12 + 12 + 12 + 12 = _____

4 × 12 = ____   12 + 12 + 12 + 12 + 12 + 12 + 12 + 12 + 12 + 12 = _____

5 × 12 = ____   12 + 12 + 12 + 12 + 12 + 12 + 12 + 12 + 12 + 12 + 12 + 12 = _____

6 × 12 = ____   12 + 12 + 12 = _____

7 × 12 = ____   12 + 12 = _____

8 × 12 = ____   12 + 12 + 12 + 12 + 12 + 12 + 12 + 12 + 12 = _____

9 × 12 = ____   12 + 12 + 12 + 12 = _____

10 × 12 = ____   12 + 0 = _____

11 × 12 = ____   12 + 12 + 12 + 12 + 12 + 12 = _____

12 × 12 = ____   12 + 12 + 12 + 12 + 12 + 12 + 12 + 12 + 12 + 12 + 12 = _____

Twelve Times Table

1. Multiply. Use the key to colour the products.

Colour Key
0 - red
12 - orange
24 - yellow
36 - light green
48 - green
60 - light blue
72 - dark blue
84 - purple
96 - pink
108 - brown
120 - grey
132 - black
144 - gold

$$\begin{array}{r} 3 \\ \times\ 12 \\ \hline \end{array}$$

$$\begin{array}{r} 0 \\ \times\ 12 \\ \hline \end{array}$$

$$\begin{array}{r} 8 \\ \times\ 12 \\ \hline \end{array}$$

$$\begin{array}{r} 9 \\ \times\ 12 \\ \hline \end{array}$$

$$\begin{array}{r} 11 \\ \times\ 12 \\ \hline \end{array}$$

$$\begin{array}{r} 5 \\ \times\ 12 \\ \hline \end{array}$$

$$\begin{array}{r} 1 \\ \times\ 12 \\ \hline \end{array}$$

$$\begin{array}{r} 2 \\ \times\ 12 \\ \hline \end{array}$$

$$\begin{array}{r} 7 \\ \times\ 12 \\ \hline \end{array}$$

$$\begin{array}{r} 6 \\ \times\ 12 \\ \hline \end{array}$$

$$\begin{array}{r} 12 \\ \times\ 10 \\ \hline \end{array}$$

$$\begin{array}{r} 12 \\ \times\ 8 \\ \hline \end{array}$$

$$\begin{array}{r} 12 \\ \times\ 2 \\ \hline \end{array}$$

$$\begin{array}{r} 12 \\ \times\ 4 \\ \hline \end{array}$$

$$\begin{array}{r} 12 \\ \times\ 9 \\ \hline \end{array}$$

$$\begin{array}{r} 12 \\ \times\ 11 \\ \hline \end{array}$$

$$\begin{array}{r} 12 \\ \times\ 3 \\ \hline \end{array}$$

$$\begin{array}{r} 12 \\ \times\ 6 \\ \hline \end{array}$$

$$\begin{array}{r} 4 \\ \times\ 12 \\ \hline \end{array}$$

$$\begin{array}{r} 12 \\ \times\ 12 \\ \hline \end{array}$$

$$\begin{array}{r} 12 \\ \times\ 5 \\ \hline \end{array}$$

$$\begin{array}{r} 12 \\ \times\ 7 \\ \hline \end{array}$$

$$\begin{array}{r} 12 \\ \times\ 1 \\ \hline \end{array}$$

$$\begin{array}{r} 12 \\ \times\ 0 \\ \hline \end{array}$$

Tip for Multiplying by 12
Remember that every fact has a twin!
So 3 × 12 has a twin called 12 × 3.
If you know the fact for 3, multiplying becomes easy!

Remember to practice skip counting by 12s!

Twelve Times Table (continued)

2. Find the product.

Watch out! Not all of the letters are used in the answer.

A	B	D	E	I
$7 \times 12 =$ ____	$12 \times 12 =$ ____	$5 \times 12 =$ ____	$3 \times 12 =$ ____	$11 \times 12 =$ ____

K	M	S	T	W
$6 \times 12 =$ ____	$2 \times 12 =$ ____	$8 \times 12 =$ ____	$9 \times 12 =$ ____	$10 \times 12 =$ ____

Math Riddle: **What did the spider do on the computer?**

___ ___ / ___ ___ ___ ___ / ___ / ___ ___ ___ ___ ___ ___ ___ !
132 108 24 84 60 36 84 120 36 144 96 132 108 36

3. Find the missing factor.

$7 \times$ ____ $= 84$	$2 \times$ ____ $= 24$	$3 \times$ ____ $= 36$	____ $\times 12 = 96$
____ $\times 4 = 48$	$9 \times$ ____ $= 108$	__ $\times 12 = 60$	$12 \times$ ____ $= 132$
$10 \times$ ____ $= 120$	____ $\times 12 = 48$	____ $\times 12 = 72$	____ $\times 12 = 24$
____ $\times 12 = 12$	$12 \times$ ____ $= 60$	__ $\times 12 = 0$	____ $\times 12 = 144$

Multiply by 10, 11, and 12

1. Find the product. Colour odd products red. Colour even products blue.

9 × 12	11 × 10	9 × 11	4 × 10	4 × 12
3 × 10	5 × 11	11 × 12	7 × 10	6 × 11
5 × 10	2 × 12	7 × 11	10 × 11	3 × 12
12 × 10	5 × 12	2 × 10	6 × 12	8 × 10
3 × 11	9 × 10	12 × 11	6 × 10	8 × 11
12 × 12	4 × 11	7 × 12	11 × 11	8 × 12

Math Riddle: Multiplication Facts for 10, 11, and 12

How do you greet a two-headed alien?

___ ___ ___ ___ | ___ ___ | ___ ___ ___ ___ | ___ ___ ___ !
72 84 55 96 | 20 90 | 121 96 96 20 | 48 90 77

___ ___ ___ ___ | ___ ___ | ___ ___ ___ ___ | ___ ___ ___ !
72 84 55 96 | 20 90 | 121 96 96 20 | 48 90 77

A	C	D	E	G
12 × 10	5 × 11	11 × 10	8 × 12	6 × 11
I	**L**	**M**	**N**	**O**
7 × 12	10 × 10	11 × 11	6 × 12	9 × 10
P	**R**	**T**	**U**	**Y**
3 × 11	9 × 12	2 × 10	7 × 11	4 × 12

Watch out! Not all of the letters are used in the answer.

Math Blaster—Multiplication Challenge 1

Multiply. How quickly can you solve these questions? Time yourself.

1. 2 × 7 = _____

2. 3 × 6 = _____

3. 11 × 4 = _____

4. 2 × 8 = _____

5. 0 × 9 = _____

6. 8 × 6 = _____

7. 9 × 10 = _____

8. 7 × 6 = _____

9. 8 × 8 = _____

10. 6 × 9 = _____

11. 4 × 4 = _____

12. 5 × 1 = _____

13. 4 × 7 = _____

14. 9 × 2 = _____

15. 7 × 3 = _____

16. 0 × 11 = _____

17. 1 × 2 = _____

18. 6 × 8 = _____

19. 5 × 7 = _____

20. 10 × 10 = _____

21. 9 × 5 = _____

22. 8 × 4 = _____

23. 9 × 12 = _____

24. 1 × 9 = _____

25. 7 × 5 = _____

26. 0 × 6 = _____

27. 8 × 2 = _____

28. 4 × 1 = _____

29. 6 × 6 = _____

30. 5 × 8 = _____

31. 8 × 3 = _____

32. 3 × 3 = _____

33. 5 × 6 = _____

34. 1 × 5 = _____

35. 7 × 7 = _____

36. 9 × 9 = _____

37. 2 × 5 = _____

38. 0 × 4 = _____

39. 9 × 3 = _____

40. 12 × 12 = _____

41. 12 × 7 = _____

42. 7 × 2 = _____

43. 9 × 11 = _____

44. 11 × 10 = _____

45. 2 × 0 = _____

46. 4 × 5 = _____

47. 6 × 7 = _____

48. 8 × 11 = _____

49. 3 × 8 = _____

50. 10 × 10 = _____

Time

_____

Math Blaster Score

_____
50

Math Blaster—Multiplication Challenge 2

Multiply. How quickly can you solve these questions? Time yourself.

1. $6 \times 3 =$ _____

2. $8 \times 2 =$ _____

3. $10 \times 5 =$ _____

4. $0 \times 1 =$ _____

5. $7 \times 4 =$ _____

6. $6 \times 7 =$ _____

7. $11 \times 4 =$ _____

8. $3 \times 5 =$ _____

9. $2 \times 2 =$ _____

10. $6 \times 11 =$ _____

11. $9 \times 9 =$ _____

12. $4 \times 5 =$ _____

13. $5 \times 5 =$ _____

14. $3 \times 7 =$ _____

15. $9 \times 8 =$ _____

16. $2 \times 7 =$ _____

17. $2 \times 6 =$ _____

18. $11 \times 3 =$ _____

19. $9 \times 3 =$ _____

20. $10 \times 9 =$ _____

21. $9 \times 1 =$ _____

22. $8 \times 7 =$ _____

23. $2 \times 1 =$ _____

24. $9 \times 7 =$ _____

25. $4 \times 6 =$ _____

26. $6 \times 2 =$ _____

27. $7 \times 8 =$ _____

28. $6 \times 5 =$ _____

29. $12 \times 1 =$ _____

30. $7 \times 9 =$ _____

31. $4 \times 3 =$ _____

32. $3 \times 8 =$ _____

33. $1 \times 6 =$ _____

34. $5 \times 3 =$ _____

35. $6 \times 9 =$ _____

36. $0 \times 7 =$ _____

37. $12 \times 10 =$ _____

38. $7 \times 2 =$ _____

39. $8 \times 5 =$ _____

40. $9 \times 6 =$ _____

41. $12 \times 6 =$ _____

42. $7 \times 11 =$ _____

43. $9 \times 9 =$ _____

44. $11 \times 6 =$ _____

45. $2 \times 11 =$ _____

46. $4 \times 0 =$ _____

47. $6 \times 1 =$ _____

48. $8 \times 12 =$ _____

49. $2 \times 10 =$ _____

50. $10 \times 7 =$ _____

Time

_____

Math Blaster Score

50

Math Blaster—Multiplication Challenge 3

Multiply. How quickly can you solve these questions? Time yourself.

1. 2 × 6 = _____
2. 3 × 3 = _____
3. 9 × 6 = _____
4. 10 × 9 = _____
5. 9 × 9 = _____
6. 2 × 8 = _____
7. 4 × 12 = _____
8. 6 × 11 = _____
9. 5 × 1 = _____
10. 3 × 4 = _____
11. 4 × 6 = _____
12. 6 × 11 = _____
13. 0 × 8 = _____
14. 11 × 5 = _____
15. 1 × 2 = _____
16. 7 × 6 = _____
17. 12 × 7 = _____
18. 1 × 1 = _____
19. 8 × 10 = _____
20. 10 × 12 = _____

21. 5 × 12 = _____
22. 10 × 3 = _____
23. 9 × 8 = _____
24. 9 × 7 = _____
25. 4 × 11 = _____
26. 1 × 2 = _____
27. 2 × 11 = _____
28. 8 × 1 = _____
29. 3 × 1 = _____
30. 4 × 4 = _____
31. 5 × 6 = _____
32. 7 × 5 = _____
33. 4 × 9 = _____
34. 0 × 10 = _____
35. 12 × 3 = _____
36. 8 × 6 = _____
37. 7 × 10 = _____
38. 3 × 11 = _____
39. 6 × 6 = _____
40. 9 × 12 = _____

41. 12 × 3 = _____
42. 7 × 2 = _____
43. 11 × 9 = _____
44. 10 × 10 = _____
45. 5 × 10 = _____
46. 2 × 11 = _____
47. 6 × 6 = _____
48. 8 × 11 = _____
49. 3 × 10 = _____
50. 10 × 4 = _____

Time

_____

Math Blaster Score

50

Math Blaster—Multiplication Challenge 4

Multiply. How quickly can you solve these questions? Time yourself.

1. 12 × 12 = _____

2. 9 × 3 = _____

3. 4 × 7 = _____

4. 7 × 2 = _____

5. 3 × 10 = _____

6. 2 × 4 = _____

7. 5 × 8 = _____

8. 8 × 11 = _____

9. 10 × 9 = _____

10. 3 × 9 = _____

11. 5 × 7 = _____

12. 5 × 2 = _____

13. 11 × 10 = _____

14. 0 × 9 = _____

15. 6 × 5 = _____

16. 5 × 5 = _____

17. 11 × 12 = _____

18. 2 × 7 = _____

19. 7 × 4 = _____

20. 1 × 11 = _____

21. 9 × 5 = _____

22. 4 × 9 = _____

23. 7 × 3 = _____

24. 8 × 8 = _____

25. 4 × 12 = _____

26. 1 × 7 = _____

27. 2 × 10 = _____

28. 8 × 12 = _____

29. 10 × 10 = _____

30. 0 × 2 = _____

31. 2 × 2 = _____

32. 9 × 8 = _____

33. 4 × 6 = _____

34. 8 × 7 = _____

35. 11 × 11 = _____

36. 3 × 8 = _____

37. 5 × 1 = _____

38. 3 × 6 = _____

39. 5 × 12 = _____

40. 7 × 10 = _____

41. 12 × 7 = _____

42. 7 × 2 = _____

43. 9 × 11 = _____

44. 10 × 11 = _____

45. 2 × 0 = _____

46. 3 × 5 = _____

47. 6 × 7 = _____

48. 11 × 7 = _____

49. 3 × 8 = _____

50. 9 × 10 = _____

Time

_____

Math Blaster Score

_____

50

Multiply. How quickly can you solve these questions? Time yourself.

1. 11 × 12 = _____

2. 8 × 3 = _____

3. 3 × 7 = _____

4. 6 × 2 = _____

5. 2 × 10 = _____

6. 1 × 4 = _____

7. 4 × 8 = _____

8. 7 × 11 = _____

9. 9 × 9 = _____

10. 2 × 9 = _____

11. 4 × 7 = _____

12. 4 × 2 = _____

13. 10 × 10 = _____

14. 1 × 9 = _____

15. 5 × 5 = _____

16. 4 × 5 = _____

17. 10 × 12 = _____

18. 0 × 7 = _____

19. 6 × 4 = _____

20. 0 × 11 = _____

21. 8 × 5 = _____

22. 3 × 9 = _____

23. 6 × 3 = _____

24. 7 × 8 = _____

25. 3 × 12 = _____

26. 1 × 7 = _____

27. 1 × 10 = _____

28. 7 × 12 = _____

29. 9 × 10 = _____

30. 12 × 2 = _____

31. 11 × 2 = _____

32. 8 × 8 = _____

33. 3 × 6 = _____

34. 7 × 7 = _____

35. 10 × 11 = _____

36. 2 × 8 = _____

37. 5 × 1 = _____

38. 2 × 6 = _____

39. 4 × 12 = _____

40. 6 × 10 = _____

41. 12 × 12 = _____

42. 2 × 7 = _____

43. 10 × 8 = _____

44. 5 × 10 = _____

45. 4 × 5 = _____

46. 6 × 12 = _____

47. 9 × 12 = _____

48. 8 × 8 = _____

49. 3 × 3 = _____

50. 12 × 11 = _____

Time

_____

Math Blaster Score

_____ / 50

Math Blaster 1—Multiplying by 1 to 6

4	4	6	7	4	12	10
× 6	× 4	× 5	× 6	× 1	× 3	× 2

3	11	7	4	8	7	9
× 1	× 2	× 2	× 5	× 3	× 4	× 2

6	6	12	1	5	8
× 6	× 3	× 2	× 4	× 5	× 5

Math Blaster Score

_____
20

Math Blaster 2—Multiplying by 1 to 6

4	5	3	4	9	7	9
× 1	× 2	× 5	× 6	× 2	× 1	× 4

4	2	5	8	5	6	8
× 3	× 6	× 5	× 6	× 3	× 4	× 3

10	7	12	1	6	11
× 4	× 3	× 5	× 1	× 2	× 2

Math Blaster Score

_____
20

Math Blaster 3—Multiplying by 1 to 6

$$
\begin{array}{ccccccc}
11 & 5 & 9 & 12 & 1 & 8 & 10 \\
\times\ 6 & \times\ 3 & \times\ 5 & \times\ 4 & \times\ 2 & \times\ 3 & \times\ 2 \\
\end{array}
$$

$$
\begin{array}{ccccccc}
6 & 8 & 2 & 4 & 3 & 4 & 7 \\
\times\ 3 & \times\ 5 & \times\ 1 & \times\ 4 & \times\ 3 & \times\ 5 & \times\ 6 \\
\end{array}
$$

$$
\begin{array}{cccccc}
6 & 11 & 5 & 9 & 8 & 6 \\
\times\ 2 & \times\ 3 & \times\ 5 & \times\ 6 & \times\ 1 & \times\ 4 \\
\end{array}
$$

Math Blaster Score ___ / 20

Math Blaster 4—Multiplying by 1 to 6

$$
\begin{array}{ccccccc}
3 & 5 & 3 & 8 & 3 & 12 & 10 \\
\times\ 1 & \times\ 6 & \times\ 2 & \times\ 4 & \times\ 3 & \times\ 5 & \times\ 5 \\
\end{array}
$$

$$
\begin{array}{ccccccc}
9 & 2 & 11 & 10 & 8 & 6 & 7 \\
\times\ 1 & \times\ 1 & \times\ 4 & \times\ 6 & \times\ 5 & \times\ 3 & \times\ 3 \\
\end{array}
$$

$$
\begin{array}{cccccc}
5 & 7 & 6 & 10 & 9 & 8 \\
\times\ 4 & \times\ 2 & \times\ 5 & \times\ 3 & \times\ 2 & \times\ 6 \\
\end{array}
$$

Math Blaster Score ___ / 20

Math Blaster 5—Multiplying by 1 to 6

6	3	11	7	12	9	9
× 4	× 2	× 1	× 6	× 3	× 2	× 5

5	3	6	4	10	4	7
× 6	× 4	× 5	× 2	× 3	× 5	× 2

4	1	2	2	8	12
× 4	× 2	× 5	× 3	× 1	× 6

Math Blaster Score

_____
20

Math Blaster 6—Multiplying by 1 to 6

3	5	11	5	8	1	8
× 4	× 3	× 5	× 1	× 6	× 2	× 4

6	8	6	3	7	5	10
× 6	× 1	× 5	× 3	× 2	× 4	× 4

2	3	12	8	12	9
× 5	× 2	× 6	× 3	× 1	× 4

Math Blaster Score

_____
20

Math Blaster 7—Multiplying by 1 to 6

9 × 2	11 × 3	7 × 6	8 × 4	2 × 1	4 × 3	2 × 5
6 × 2	12 × 4	7 × 3	5 × 2	12 × 6	1 × 1	6 × 5
10 × 1	5 × 6	10 × 5	1 × 3	6 × 4	9 × 3	

Math Blaster Score

____
20

Math Blaster 8—Multiplying by 1 to 6

3 × 4	5 × 3	3 × 2	11 × 6	6 × 5	10 × 4	8 × 4
5 × 4	4 × 6	12 × 5	4 × 2	3 × 3	3 × 1	7 × 3
5 × 2	10 × 2	1 × 6	8 × 5	9 × 3	4 × 3	

Math Blaster Score

____
20

Math Blaster 9—Multiplying by 1 to 6

6	11	5	7	6	12	8
× 4	× 2	× 1	× 5	× 6	× 2	× 6

3	11	3	8	4	9	7
× 2	× 3	× 6	× 2	× 3	× 4	× 4

10	2	9	8	12	9
× 5	× 4	× 2	× 3	× 6	× 5

Math Blaster Score

___
20

Math Blaster 10—Multiplying by 1 to 6

5	6	12	2	1	7	10
× 5	× 6	× 3	× 2	× 4	× 2	× 2

6	2	8	4	2	10	3
× 2	× 1	× 3	× 5	× 6	× 1	× 4

9	11	4	7	5	9
× 6	× 5	× 3	× 4	× 2	× 4

Math Blaster Score

___
20

Math Blaster 1—Multiplying by 7 to 12

| $\begin{array}{r} 4 \\ \times\ 12 \\ \hline \end{array}$ | $\begin{array}{r} 8 \\ \times\ 10 \\ \hline \end{array}$ | $\begin{array}{r} 6 \\ \times\ 11 \\ \hline \end{array}$ | $\begin{array}{r} 7 \\ \times\ 7 \\ \hline \end{array}$ | $\begin{array}{r} 10 \\ \times\ 11 \\ \hline \end{array}$ | $\begin{array}{r} 9 \\ \times\ 8 \\ \hline \end{array}$ | $\begin{array}{r} 11 \\ \times\ 9 \\ \hline \end{array}$ |

| $\begin{array}{r} 3 \\ \times\ 7 \\ \hline \end{array}$ | $\begin{array}{r} 12 \\ \times\ 10 \\ \hline \end{array}$ | $\begin{array}{r} 9 \\ \times\ 9 \\ \hline \end{array}$ | $\begin{array}{r} 6 \\ \times\ 12 \\ \hline \end{array}$ | $\begin{array}{r} 8 \\ \times\ 9 \\ \hline \end{array}$ | $\begin{array}{r} 2 \\ \times\ 8 \\ \hline \end{array}$ | $\begin{array}{r} 7 \\ \times\ 11 \\ \hline \end{array}$ |

| $\begin{array}{r} 5 \\ \times\ 11 \\ \hline \end{array}$ | $\begin{array}{r} 8 \\ \times\ 12 \\ \hline \end{array}$ | $\begin{array}{r} 4 \\ \times\ 10 \\ \hline \end{array}$ | $\begin{array}{r} 9 \\ \times\ 7 \\ \hline \end{array}$ | $\begin{array}{r} 7 \\ \times\ 12 \\ \hline \end{array}$ | $\begin{array}{r} 3 \\ \times\ 8 \\ \hline \end{array}$ |

Math Blaster Score

——— 20

Math Blaster 2—Multiplying by 7 to 12

| $\begin{array}{r} 8 \\ \times\ 7 \\ \hline \end{array}$ | $\begin{array}{r} 8 \\ \times\ 9 \\ \hline \end{array}$ | $\begin{array}{r} 9 \\ \times\ 11 \\ \hline \end{array}$ | $\begin{array}{r} 7 \\ \times\ 7 \\ \hline \end{array}$ | $\begin{array}{r} 10 \\ \times\ 8 \\ \hline \end{array}$ | $\begin{array}{r} 6 \\ \times\ 12 \\ \hline \end{array}$ | $\begin{array}{r} 10 \\ \times\ 10 \\ \hline \end{array}$ |

| $\begin{array}{r} 4 \\ \times\ 11 \\ \hline \end{array}$ | $\begin{array}{r} 7 \\ \times\ 10 \\ \hline \end{array}$ | $\begin{array}{r} 3 \\ \times\ 8 \\ \hline \end{array}$ | $\begin{array}{r} 10 \\ \times\ 12 \\ \hline \end{array}$ | $\begin{array}{r} 9 \\ \times\ 7 \\ \hline \end{array}$ | $\begin{array}{r} 6 \\ \times\ 9 \\ \hline \end{array}$ | $\begin{array}{r} 6 \\ \times\ 7 \\ \hline \end{array}$ |

| $\begin{array}{r} 12 \\ \times\ 9 \\ \hline \end{array}$ | $\begin{array}{r} 4 \\ \times\ 8 \\ \hline \end{array}$ | $\begin{array}{r} 11 \\ \times\ 7 \\ \hline \end{array}$ | $\begin{array}{r} 5 \\ \times\ 11 \\ \hline \end{array}$ | $\begin{array}{r} 2 \\ \times\ 10 \\ \hline \end{array}$ | $\begin{array}{r} 8 \\ \times\ 12 \\ \hline \end{array}$ |

Math Blaster Score

——— 20

Math Blaster 3—Multiplying by 7 to 12

8 × 11	12 × 10	10 × 9	8 × 8	6 × 7	2 × 11	9 × 9
3 × 10	10 × 7	10 × 12	6 × 12	5 × 7	11 × 8	4 × 9
7 × 7	6 × 8	11 × 11	9 × 12	9 × 11	12 × 9	

Math Blaster Score

_____
20

Math Blaster 4—Multiplying by 7 to 12

9 × 8	10 × 8	7 × 10	6 × 9	11 × 7	3 × 11	1 × 12
9 × 10	5 × 8	7 × 12	4 × 9	6 × 8	2 × 7	5 × 10
1 × 10	5 × 12	12 × 11	2 × 8	8 × 9	4 × 10	

Math Blaster Score

_____
20

Math Blaster 5—Multiplying by 7 to 12

4	6	8	10	8	6	7
× 7	× 10	× 9	× 10	× 11	× 12	× 11

11	5	9	6	12	10	2
× 8	× 9	× 10	× 7	10	× 7	× 11

10	3	7	12	9	7
× 12	× 12	× 9	× 7	× 8	× 8

Math Blaster Score

_____

20

Math Blaster 6—Multiplying by 7 to 12

9	4	8	6	7	10	12
× 7	× 10	× 8	× 12	× 11	× 7	× 7

6	11	4	3	2	1	7
× 7	× 10	× 9	× 8	× 8	× 12	× 9

5	3	5	12	8	9
× 11	× 12	× 8	× 9	× 10	× 11

Math Blaster Score

_____

20

Math Blaster 7—Multiplying by 7 to 12

$$\begin{array}{r} 9 \\ \times\ 10 \\ \hline \end{array} \qquad \begin{array}{r} 7 \\ \times\ 8 \\ \hline \end{array} \qquad \begin{array}{r} 6 \\ \times\ 7 \\ \hline \end{array} \qquad \begin{array}{r} 10 \\ \times\ 10 \\ \hline \end{array} \qquad \begin{array}{r} 3 \\ \times\ 8 \\ \hline \end{array} \qquad \begin{array}{r} 6 \\ \times\ 9 \\ \hline \end{array} \qquad \begin{array}{r} 8 \\ \times\ 9 \\ \hline \end{array}$$

$$\begin{array}{r} 7 \\ \times\ 7 \\ \hline \end{array} \qquad \begin{array}{r} 12 \\ \times\ 9 \\ \hline \end{array} \qquad \begin{array}{r} 8 \\ \times\ 12 \\ \hline \end{array} \qquad \begin{array}{r} 3 \\ \times\ 11 \\ \hline \end{array} \qquad \begin{array}{r} 1 \\ \times\ 8 \\ \hline \end{array} \qquad \begin{array}{r} 9 \\ \times\ 7 \\ \hline \end{array} \qquad \begin{array}{r} 12 \\ \times\ 10 \\ \hline \end{array}$$

$$\begin{array}{r} 6 \\ \times\ 8 \\ \hline \end{array} \qquad \begin{array}{r} 11 \\ \times\ 9 \\ \hline \end{array} \qquad \begin{array}{r} 2 \\ \times\ 12 \\ \hline \end{array} \qquad \begin{array}{r} 7 \\ \times\ 9 \\ \hline \end{array} \qquad \begin{array}{r} 4 \\ \times\ 11 \\ \hline \end{array} \qquad \begin{array}{r} 5 \\ \times\ 10 \\ \hline \end{array}$$

Math Blaster Score

_____
20

Math Blaster 8—Multiplying by 7 to 12

$$\begin{array}{r} 6 \\ \times\ 11 \\ \hline \end{array} \qquad \begin{array}{r} 8 \\ \times\ 8 \\ \hline \end{array} \qquad \begin{array}{r} 7 \\ \times\ 9 \\ \hline \end{array} \qquad \begin{array}{r} 10 \\ \times\ 7 \\ \hline \end{array} \qquad \begin{array}{r} 2 \\ \times\ 10 \\ \hline \end{array} \qquad \begin{array}{r} 11 \\ \times\ 7 \\ \hline \end{array} \qquad \begin{array}{r} 6 \\ \times\ 12 \\ \hline \end{array}$$

$$\begin{array}{r} 4 \\ \times\ 10 \\ \hline \end{array} \qquad \begin{array}{r} 8 \\ \times\ 10 \\ \hline \end{array} \qquad \begin{array}{r} 10 \\ \times\ 9 \\ \hline \end{array} \qquad \begin{array}{r} 6 \\ \times\ 8 \\ \hline \end{array} \qquad \begin{array}{r} 1 \\ \times\ 7 \\ \hline \end{array} \qquad \begin{array}{r} 5 \\ \times\ 12 \\ \hline \end{array} \qquad \begin{array}{r} 4 \\ \times\ 9 \\ \hline \end{array}$$

$$\begin{array}{r} 12 \\ \times\ 7 \\ \hline \end{array} \qquad \begin{array}{r} 5 \\ \times\ 12 \\ \hline \end{array} \qquad \begin{array}{r} 7 \\ \times\ 7 \\ \hline \end{array} \qquad \begin{array}{r} 4 \\ \times\ 11 \\ \hline \end{array} \qquad \begin{array}{r} 3 \\ \times\ 8 \\ \hline \end{array} \qquad \begin{array}{r} 9 \\ \times\ 9 \\ \hline \end{array}$$

Math Blaster Score

_____
20

Math Blaster 9—Multiplying by 7 to 12

2 × 7	7 × 12	9 × 9	8 × 8	6 × 11	10 × 11	10 × 9
8 × 11	3 × 11	6 × 8	11 × 12	5 × 7	2 × 8	4 × 9
4 × 10	12 × 7	7 × 8	4 × 12	1 × 10	9 × 10	

Math Blaster Score

_____
20

Math Blaster 10—Multiplying by 7 to 12

9 × 9	4 × 12	11 × 8	9 × 11	8 × 10	3 × 7	1 × 10
10 × 7	7 × 8	2 × 7	8 × 12	9 × 10	10 × 11	7 × 7
5 × 8	2 × 10	6 × 12	3 × 9	10 × 9	11 × 12	

Math Blaster Score

_____
20

Math Blaster 1—Multiplying by 1 to 12

7	4	9	5	8	2	10
× 5	× 6	× 9	× 3	× 2	× 4	× 7

4	9	12	4	7	10	5
× 9	× 10	× 6	× 4	× 8	× 1	× 8

6	10	3	2	12	11
× 5	× 2	× 7	× 5	× 12	× 11

Math Blaster Score

_____ / 20

Math Blaster 2—Multiplying by 1 to 12

8	7	11	3	9	6	4
× 5	× 6	× 10	× 4	× 8	× 6	× 9

10	12	6	6	3	8	3
× 10	× 1	× 4	× 2	× 11	× 7	× 8

5	6	4	1	2	7
× 2	× 7	× 12	× 5	× 2	× 3

Math Blaster Score

_____ / 20

Math Blaster 3—Multiplying by 1 to 12

9	4	10	11	8	12	8
× 3	× 1	× 6	× 11	× 7	× 9	× 10

9	11	6	8	4	11	5
× 4	× 5	× 8	× 4	× 2	× 8	× 7

9	10	7	6	5	2
× 2	× 12	× 3	× 9	× 5	× 6

Math Blaster Score

_____
20

Math Blaster 4—Multiplying by 1 to 12

7	5	4	6	3	12	7
× 9	× 12	× 4	× 8	× 7	× 3	× 10

2	11	2	6	10	9	8
× 5	× 1	× 7	× 5	× 8	× 6	× 5

3	3	7	5	7	1
× 2	× 6	× 11	× 4	× 2	× 8

Math Blaster Score

_____
20

Math Blaster 5--Multiplying by 1 to 12

10	1	9	6	5	3	7
× 9	× 2	× 8	× 4	× 7	× 3	× 9

3	11	3	8	5	6	8
× 4	× 9	× 5	× 6	× 9	× 10	× 12

7	10	6	7	12	9
× 3	× 12	× 11	× 6	× 2	× 1

Math Blaster Score

_____

20

Math Blaster 6—Multiplying by 1 to 12

7	12	5	3	9	6	2
× 5	× 12	× 10	× 9	× 7	× 8	× 8

10	4	9	3	10	5	7
× 4	× 4	× 9	× 6	× 2	× 9	× 11

12	1	10	11	5	7
× 3	× 12	× 3	× 8	× 1	× 6

Math Blaster Score

_____

20

Math Blaster 7—Multiplying by 1 to 12

4 × 10	12 × 2	9 × 7	9 × 5	10 × 12	9 × 6	11 × 9
4 × 1	5 × 12	2 × 3	9 × 8	6 × 7	10 × 4	3 × 11
6 × 3	1 × 9	11 × 8	7 × 3	5 × 6	2 × 7	**Math Blaster Score** ___ 20

Math Blaster 8—Multiplying by 1 to 12

6 × 7	12 × 7	4 × 9	5 × 11	3 × 8	5 × 12	9 × 8
10 × 5	5 × 1	7 × 7	3 × 4	11 × 6	2 × 3	12 × 11
6 × 9	2 × 10	8 × 2	12 × 8	9 × 9	4 × 10	**Math Blaster Score** ___ 20

Math Blaster 9—Multiplying by 1 to 12

2 × 10	1 × 4	6 × 9	9 × 5	8 × 8	12 × 9	10 × 7
1 × 5	6 × 7	7 × 8	4 × 9	11 × 6	9 × 8	5 × 9
8 × 3	10 × 11	3 × 2	2 × 1	12 × 12	2 × 7	Math Blaster Score —— 20

Math Blaster 10—Multiplying by 1 to 12

11 × 9	7 × 7	4 × 8	6 × 9	5 × 5	10 × 6	8 × 11
6 × 4	4 × 9	12 × 2	10 × 4	5 × 9	3 × 3	9 × 8
10 × 3	2 × 5	11 × 1	4 × 7	1 × 10	9 × 12	Math Blaster Score —— 20

Multiply by Tens

You can use sticks to multiply by tens.

2 × 30 =
Make 2 groups of 3 tens.

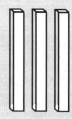 

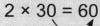 = 10

2 × 30 = 2 × 3 tens = 6 tens = 60   So, 2 × 30 = 60.
What pattern do you see?   2 × 3 = 6
                              2 × 30 = 60

1. Draw a stick for each ten. Then multiply.

a) 2 × 40 = _____   b) 3 × 80 = _____

2. Use the pattern to multiply.

a) 5 × 1 = _____   b) 7 × 4 = _____   c) 3 × 9 = _____

   5 × 10 = _____   7 × 40 = _____   3 × 90 = _____

Multiply by Hundreds

You can use squares to multiply by hundreds.

 = 100

3 × 200 =
Make 3 groups of 2 hundreds.

3 × 200 = 3 × 2 hundreds = 6 hundreds = 600   So, 3 × 200 = 600.

What pattern do you see?   3 × 2 = 6

3 × 20 = 60

3 × 200 = 600

---

1. Draw a H square for each hundred. Then multiply.

a) 4 × 200 = _____   b) 3 × 500 = _____

2. Use the pattern to multiply.

a) 7 × 6 = _____   b) 4 × 5 = _____   c) 6 × 4 = _____

7 × 60 = _____   4 × 50 = _____   6 × 40 = _____

7 × 600 = _____   4 × 500 = _____   6 × 400 = _____

Multiply by Thousands

You can use T squares to multiply by thousands.

$\boxed{T}$ = 1000

4 × 2000 =
Make 4 groups of 2 thousands.

4 × 2000 = 4 × 2 thousands = 8 thousands = 8000   So, 4 × 2000 = 8000.
What pattern do you see?   4 × 2 = 8
                             4 × 20 = 80
                             4 × 200 = 800
                             4 × 2000 = 8000

1. Draw a T square for each thousand. Then multiply.

a) 4 × 4000 = _____   b) 8 × 3000 = _____

c) 5 × 1000 = _____   d) 7 × 3000 = _____

Multiply Multiples of 10, 100, and 1000

Multiply $7 \times 5000 =$ _____

7×5 ones = <u>35</u> ones = **35**

7×5 tens = <u>35</u> tens = **350**

7×5 hundreds = <u>35</u> hundreds = **3500**

7×5 thousands = <u>35</u> thousands = **35 000**

So $7 \times 5000 =$ **35 000**.

1. Use multiplication facts and patterns to help you multiply.

a) $5 \times 4 =$ _____

   $5 \times 40 =$ _____

   $5 \times 400 =$ _____

   $5 \times 4000 =$ _____

b) $8 \times 7 =$ _____

   $8 \times 70 =$ _____

   $8 \times 700 =$ _____

   $8 \times 7000 =$ _____

c) $9 \times 2 =$ _____

   $9 \times 20 =$ _____

   $9 \times 200 =$ _____

   $9 \times 2000 =$ _____

d) $6 \times 6 =$ _____

   $6 \times 60 =$ _____

   $6 \times 600 =$ _____

   $6 \times 6000 =$ _____

e) $4 \times 7 =$ _____

   $4 \times 70 =$ _____

   $4 \times 700 =$ _____

   $4 \times 7000 =$ _____

f) $3 \times 4 =$ _____

   $3 \times 40 =$ _____

   $3 \times 400 =$ _____

   $3 \times 4000 =$ _____

g) $6 \times 8 =$ _____

   $6 \times 80 =$ _____

   $6 \times 800 =$ _____

   $6 \times 8000 =$ _____

h) $2 \times 5 =$ _____

   $2 \times 50 =$ _____

   $2 \times 500 =$ _____

   $2 \times 5000 =$ _____

l) $7 \times 5 =$ _____

   $7 \times 50 =$ _____

   $7 \times 500 =$ _____

   $7 \times 5000 =$ _____

Multiply Multiples of 10, 100, and 1000 (continued)

2. Use the pattern to multiply.

a) 2 × 7 = _____

   2 × 70 = _____

   2 × 700 = _____

   2 × 7000 = _____

b) 8 × 3 = _____

   8 × 30 = _____

   8 × 300 = _____

   8 × 3000 = _____

c) 9 × 9 = _____

   9 × 90 = _____

   9 × 900 = _____

   9 × 9000 = _____

d) 5 × 3 = _____

   5 × 30 = _____

   5 × 300 = _____

   5 × 3000 = _____

e) 5 × 8 = _____

   5 × 80 = _____

   5 × 800 = _____

   5 × 8000 = _____

f) 6 × 5 = _____

   6 × 50 = _____

   6 × 500 = _____

   6 × 5000 = _____

3. Multiply.

a) 5 × 50 = _____

b) 7 × 300 = _____

c) 8 × 1000 = _____

d) 7 × 200 = _____

e) 5 × 40 = _____

f) 7 × 700 = _____

g) 5 × 500 = _____

h) 6 × 80 = _____

i) 8 × 500 = _____

j) 3 × 80 = _____

k) 2 × 1000 = _____

l) 9 × 400 = _____

m) 6 × 900 = _____

n) 4 × 30 = _____

o) 4 × 1000 = _____

p) 3 × 6000 = _____

q) 9 × 900 = _____

r) 1 × 50 = _____

Multiply Two-digit Numbers by One-digit Numbers

Step 1: Multiply the ones.	**Step 2:** Multiply the tens.
6 ones × 9 ones = 54 ones Regroup 54 as 5 tens and 4 ones.	1 ten × 9 ones = 9 tens Then add the regrouped 5 tens. 9 tens + 5 tens = 14 tens
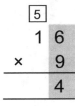	⑤ 1 6 × 9 ——— 1 4 4
	1 hundred + 4 tens + 4 ones

1. Multiply. Regroup where necessary. Hint: Make sure to line up the numbers.

```
    4 4          1 6          3 8          6 9
  ×   3        ×   4        ×   5        ×   2
  _____       _____       _____       _____


    1 7          5 4          2 7          7 6
  ×   8        ×   6        ×   9        ×   4
  _____       _____       _____       _____


    4 9          5 6          9 9          3 2
  ×   2        ×   8        ×   5        ×   2
  _____       _____       _____       _____
```

Math Blaster Score

20

2. Multiply. Regroup where necessary. Hint: Make sure to line up the numbers.

95 × 2	50 × 4	67 × 9	45 × 5
76 × 4	84 × 5	97 × 8	64 × 3
68 × 2	19 × 4	77 × 3	55 × 9
83 × 8	92 × 7	79 × 6	46 × 3
25 × 9	52 × 2	31 × 6	87 × 4

Math Blaster Score

20

3. Multiply. Regroup where necessary. Hint: Make sure to line up the numbers.

```
    38          56          78          63
  ×  2        ×  5        ×  7        ×  9
  _____       _____       _____       _____

  _____       _____       _____       _____


    42          80          97          26
  ×  6        ×  4        ×  3        ×  5
  _____       _____       _____       _____

  _____       _____       _____       _____


    74          76          55          66
  ×  8        ×  4        ×  7        ×  9
  _____       _____       _____       _____

  _____       _____       _____       _____


    32          88          91          65
  ×  4        ×  8        ×  3        ×  2
  _____       _____       _____       _____

  _____       _____       _____       _____


    27          64          43          33
  ×  5        ×  2        ×  9        ×  6
  _____       _____       _____       _____

  _____       _____       _____       _____
```

Math Blaster Score

20

4. Multiply. Regroup where necessary. Hint: Make sure to line up the numbers.

64 × 2	17 × 4	90 × 9	35 × 5
83 × 4	76 × 5	49 × 8	51 × 3
28 × 2	54 × 4	89 × 3	60 × 9
72 × 8	19 × 7	87 × 6	76 × 3
98 × 9	44 × 2	61 × 6	50 × 4

Math Blaster Score

20

Multiply Two-digit Numbers by One-digit Numbers (continued)

5. Multiply. Regroup where necessary. Hint: Make sure to line up the numbers.

$$\begin{array}{r} 26 \\ \times\ 7 \\ \hline \end{array}\qquad\begin{array}{r} 19 \\ \times\ 5 \\ \hline \end{array}\qquad\begin{array}{r} 82 \\ \times\ 5 \\ \hline \end{array}\qquad\begin{array}{r} 44 \\ \times\ 9 \\ \hline \end{array}$$

$$\begin{array}{r} 33 \\ \times\ 6 \\ \hline \end{array}\qquad\begin{array}{r} 75 \\ \times\ 4 \\ \hline \end{array}\qquad\begin{array}{r} 21 \\ \times\ 3 \\ \hline \end{array}\qquad\begin{array}{r} 57 \\ \times\ 5 \\ \hline \end{array}$$

$$\begin{array}{r} 80 \\ \times\ 8 \\ \hline \end{array}\qquad\begin{array}{r} 39 \\ \times\ 4 \\ \hline \end{array}\qquad\begin{array}{r} 17 \\ \times\ 7 \\ \hline \end{array}\qquad\begin{array}{r} 25 \\ \times\ 9 \\ \hline \end{array}$$

$$\begin{array}{r} 42 \\ \times\ 4 \\ \hline \end{array}\qquad\begin{array}{r} 98 \\ \times\ 8 \\ \hline \end{array}\qquad\begin{array}{r} 51 \\ \times\ 3 \\ \hline \end{array}\qquad\begin{array}{r} 35 \\ \times\ 2 \\ \hline \end{array}$$

$$\begin{array}{r} 17 \\ \times\ 5 \\ \hline \end{array}\qquad\begin{array}{r} 28 \\ \times\ 2 \\ \hline \end{array}\qquad\begin{array}{r} 54 \\ \times\ 9 \\ \hline \end{array}\qquad\begin{array}{r} 60 \\ \times\ 6 \\ \hline \end{array}$$

Math Blaster Score

20

Multiply Multi-digit Numbers

Step 1:	**Step 2:**	**Step 3:**
Multiply the ones.	Multiply the tens.	Multiply the hundreds.
6 ones × 5 ones	1 ten × 5 ones	3 hundreds × 5 ones
= 30 ones	= 5 tens	= 15 hundreds

Regroup 30 as 3 tens and 0 ones.	Then add the regrouped 3 tens. 5 tens + 3 tens = 8 tens	Regroup 1500 as 1 thousand and 5 hundreds.

Step 1:
```
    3
  3 1 6
×     5
  ─────
      0
```

Step 2:
```
      3
    3 1 6
  ×     5
    ─────
      8 0
```

Step 3:
```
      3
    3 1 6
  ×     5
  ───────
  1 5 8 0
```

Since there are no other thousands, write the "1" in the answer.

1. Multiply. Regroup where necessary. Check your work.

```
    3 1 4          7 0 8          4 9 7          1 3 5
  ×     3        ×     2        ×     5        ×     4
  ───────        ───────        ───────        ───────


    2 6 8          9 1 0          6 0 1          2 4 4
  ×     7        ×     6        ×     8        ×     9
  ───────        ───────        ───────        ───────
```

Multiply. Regroup where necessary. Check your work.

```
    7 5 2          2 1 4          6 7 1          8 9 0
  ×     6        ×     3        ×     4        ×     5
  _____        _____        _____        _____


  _____        _____        _____        _____


    9 2 5          6 0 7          4 5 3          5 7 0
  ×     2        ×     6        ×     3        ×     7
  _____        _____        _____        _____


  _____        _____        _____        _____


    1 6 5          8 7 5          3 4 6          6 0 4
  ×     9        ×     5        ×     8        ×     6
  _____        _____        _____        _____


  _____        _____        _____        _____


    7 3 4 1        2 7 6 4        1 5 2 8        9 0 3 2
  ×       2      ×       3      ×       5      ×       4
  _____      _____      _____      _____


  _____      _____      _____      _____


    3 4 2 0        5 4 5 1        6 1 0 9        7 8 1 5
  ×       8      ×       7      ×       6      ×       9
  _____      _____      _____      _____


  _____      _____      _____      _____
```

Math Blaster Score

_____
20

Multiply. Regroup where necessary. Check your work.

```
    5 5 3          3 0 6          8 9 0          4 1 8
  ×     6        ×     3        ×     4        ×     5
  _____        _____        _____        _____


  _____        _____        _____        _____


    7 6 1          5 4 7          1 7 8          6 3 4
  ×     2        ×     6        ×     8        ×     7
  _____        _____        _____        _____


  _____        _____        _____        _____


    2 7 5          9 8 2          1 7 4          3 2 3
  ×     9        ×     5        ×     8        ×     6
  _____        _____        _____        _____


  _____        _____        _____        _____


  5 6 7 2        2 5 3 4        3 6 7 5        1 9 0 6
  ×     2        ×     3        ×     5        ×     4
  _____        _____        _____        _____


  _____        _____        _____        _____


  8 9 4 1        4 7 8 3        9 7 5 0        4 3 8 9
  ×     8        ×     7        ×     6        ×     9
  _____        _____        _____        _____


  _____        _____        _____        _____
```

Math Blaster Score

20

Multiply Multi-digit Numbers—Challenge 3

Multiply. Regroup where necessary. Check your work.

```
  591        824        340        469
×   8      ×   3      ×   4      ×   4
_____     _____     _____     _____


_____     _____     _____     _____


  161        945        278        534
×   2      ×   6      ×   8      ×   7
_____     _____     _____     _____


_____     _____     _____     _____


  675        234        908        423
×   9      ×   5      ×   8      ×   7
_____     _____     _____     _____


_____     _____     _____     _____


 8032       4860       9541       1908
×   2      ×   3      ×   5      ×   4
_____     _____     _____     _____


_____     _____     _____     _____


 2943       5694       3628       6785
×   5      ×   7      ×   6      ×   4
_____     _____     _____     _____


_____     _____     _____     _____
```

20

Multiply Multi-digit Numbers—Challenge 4

Multiply. Regroup where necessary. Check your work.

893 × 8	104 × 4	279 × 2	385 × 5
943 × 9	217 × 8	985 × 7	539 × 3
408 × 9	743 × 5	360 × 5	173 × 6
6541 × 5	8347 × 3	1954 × 9	2083 × 6
7123 × 3	5904 × 4	4670 × 7	9082 × 9

Math Blaster Score

20

Multiply. Regroup where necessary. Check your work.

208 × 4	972 × 3	390 × 9	758 × 5
861 × 2	183 × 8	547 × 8	436 × 7
567 × 5	907 × 5	674 × 7	501 × 6
2509 × 2	1423 × 6	4786 × 5	3028 × 2
6720 × 5	8127 × 7	4305 × 6	5490 × 4

Math Blaster Score

20

Multiplication by 10, 100, and 1000—Challenge 1

Multiply.

1. $3 \times 300 =$ _____

2. $1 \times 20 =$ _____

3. $2 \times 3000 =$ _____

4. $7 \times 50 =$ _____

5. $4 \times 800 =$ _____

6. $5 \times 4000 =$ _____

7. $6 \times 20 =$ _____

8. $8 \times 100 =$ _____

9. $2 \times 7000 =$ _____

10. $3 \times 70 =$ _____

11. $9 \times 600 =$ _____

12. $7 \times 7000 =$ _____

13. $8 \times 40 =$ _____

14. $7 \times 700 =$ _____

15. $5 \times 6000 =$ _____

16. $9 \times 500 =$ _____

17. $10 \times 800 =$ _____

18. $1 \times 2000 =$ _____

19. $4 \times 80 =$ _____

20. $10 \times 50 =$ _____

21. $5 \times 100 =$ _____

22. $8 \times 300 =$ _____

23. $4 \times 50 =$ _____

24. $5 \times 1000 =$ _____

25. $4 \times 200 =$ _____

26. $1 \times 30 =$ _____

27. $3 \times 600 =$ _____

28. $7 \times 600 =$ _____

29. $10 \times 40 =$ _____

30. $1 \times 2000 =$ _____

31. $5 \times 9000 =$ _____

32. $7 \times 90 =$ _____

33. $9 \times 300 =$ _____

34. $10 \times 8000 =$ _____

35. $9 \times 70 =$ _____

36. $8 \times 700 =$ _____

37. $3 \times 7000 =$ _____

38. $2 \times 2000 =$ _____

39. $4 \times 400 =$ _____

40. $9 \times 40 =$ _____

Math Blaster Score

40

Multiply.

1.	1 × 90 = _____	**21.**	5 × 8000 = _____
2.	3 × 400 = _____	**22.**	8 × 600 = _____
3.	2 × 7000 = _____	**23.**	4 × 20 = _____
4.	7 × 80 = _____	**24.**	5 × 1000 = _____
5.	4 × 700 = _____	**25.**	4 × 900 = _____
6.	5 × 3000 = _____	**26.**	12 × 10 = _____
7.	6 × 60 = _____	**27.**	3 × 300 = _____
8.	8 × 500 = _____	**28.**	7 × 6000 = _____
9.	2 × 9000 = _____	**29.**	10 × 80 = _____
10.	3 × 60 = _____	**30.**	1 × 2000 = _____
11.	9 × 900 = _____	**31.**	5 × 500 = _____
12.	7 × 7000 = _____	**32.**	7 × 40 = _____
13.	8 × 200 = _____	**33.**	9 × 100 = _____
14.	7 × 50 = _____	**34.**	10 × 7000 = _____
15.	6 × 5000 = _____	**35.**	9 × 20 = _____
16.	4 × 500 = _____	**36.**	8 × 400 = _____
17.	10 × 70 = _____	**37.**	7 × 2000 = _____
18.	1 × 4000 = _____	**38.**	3 × 2000 = _____
19.	4 × 30 = _____	**39.**	4 × 600 = _____
20.	10 × 800 = _____	**40.**	9 × 60 = _____

Math Blaster Score

40

Multiply.

1. 1 × 30 = _____

2. 4 × 300 = _____

3. 2 × 8000 = _____

4. 9 × 50 = _____

5. 5 × 600 = _____

6. 5 × 8000 = _____

7. 6 × 40 = _____

8. 8 × 50 = _____

9. 2 × 2000 = _____

10. 3 × 7000 = _____

11. 4 × 600 = _____

12. 6 × 8000 = _____

13. 10 × 100 = _____

14. 4 × 300 = _____

15. 5 × 7000 = _____

16. 8 × 500 = _____

17. 1 × 90 = _____

18. 10 × 2000 = _____

19. 4 × 10 = _____

20. 12 × 800 = _____

21. 9 × 9000 = _____

22. 12 × 600 = _____

23. 5 × 50 = _____

24. 7 × 9000 = _____

25. 3 × 400 = _____

26. 1 × 70 = _____

27. 6 × 600 = _____

28. 7 × 400 = _____

29. 11 × 40 = _____

30. 5 × 9000 = _____

31. 8 × 100 = _____

32. 10 × 90 = _____

33. 9 × 200 = _____

34. 20 × 800 = _____

35. 7 × 70 = _____

36. 3 × 500 = _____

37. 6 × 7000 = _____

38. 11 × 2000 = _____

39. 1 × 200 = _____

40. 9 × 90 = _____

Math Blaster Score

40

Multiplication by 10, 100, and 1000—Challenge 4

Multiply.

1. 5 × 30 = _____

2. 7 × 300 = _____

3. 9 × 8000 = _____

4. 2 × 50 = _____

5. 1 × 600 = _____

6. 4 × 8000 = _____

7. 12 × 40 = _____

8. 3 × 50 = _____

9. 3 × 2000 = _____

10. 11 × 7000 = _____

11. 10 × 600 = _____

12. 3 × 8000 = _____

13. 4 × 100 = _____

14. 12 × 300 = _____

15. 4 × 7000 = _____

16. 9 × 500 = _____

17. 8 × 90 = _____

18. 11 × 2000 = _____

19. 4 × 70 = _____

20. 11 × 700 = _____

21. 4 × 9000 = _____

22. 7 × 600 = _____

23. 4 × 50 = _____

24. 4 × 9000 = _____

25. 12 × 400 = _____

26. 11 × 70 = _____

27. 2 × 600 = _____

28. 6 × 400 = _____

29. 9 × 40 = _____

30. 10 × 9000 = _____

31. 4 × 100 = _____

32. 6 × 90 = _____

33. 8 × 200 = _____

34. 7 × 8000 = _____

35. 10 × 70 = _____

36. 7 × 500 = _____

37. 2 × 7000 = _____

38. 1 × 2000 = _____

39. 3 × 200 = _____

40. 4 × 90 = _____

Math Blaster Score

_____

40

Multiplication by 10, 100, and 1000—Challenge 5

Multiply.

1. $1 \times 50 = $ _____

2. $4 \times 400 = $ _____

3. $2 \times 6000 = $ _____

4. $9 \times 40 = $ _____

5. $5 \times 900 = $ _____

6. $5 \times 3000 = $ _____

7. $6 \times 90 = $ _____

8. $10 \times 30 = $ _____

9. $3 \times 3000 = $ _____

10. $3 \times 1000 = $ _____

11. $4 \times 500 = $ _____

12. $6 \times 9000 = $ _____

13. $10 \times 200 = $ _____

14. $4 \times 700 = $ _____

15. $9 \times 7000 = $ _____

16. $3 \times 500 = $ _____

17. $12 \times 70 = $ _____

18. $11 \times 6000 = $ _____

19. $3 \times 60 = $ _____

20. $11 \times 800 = $ _____

21. $9 \times 3000 = $ _____

22. $12 \times 800 = $ _____

23. $5 \times 40 = $ _____

24. $6 \times 6000 = $ _____

25. $5 \times 500 = $ _____

26. $1 \times 80 = $ _____

27. $11 \times 600 = $ _____

28. $7 \times 100 = $ _____

29. $10 \times 10 = $ _____

30. $2 \times 9000 = $ _____

31. $5 \times 100 = $ _____

32. $11 \times 90 = $ _____

33. $9 \times 400 = $ _____

34. $12 \times 8000 = $ _____

35. $8 \times 70 = $ _____

36. $3 \times 400 = $ _____

37. $2 \times 1000 = $ _____

38. $11 \times 5000 = $ _____

39. $4 \times 600 = $ _____

40. $9 \times 80 = $ _____

Math Blaster Score

40

How Am I Doing?

Multiplying by 1 to 6 (pages 50–54)

Math Blaster Score	Math Blaster 1	Math Blaster 2	Math Blaster 3	Math Blaster 4	Math Blaster 5	Math Blaster 6	Math Blaster 7	Math Blaster 8	Math Blaster 9	Math Blaster 10
20										
19										
18										
17										
16										
15										
14										
13										
12										
11										
10										
9										
8										
7										
6										
5										
4										
3										
2										
1										

Multiplying by 7 to 12 (pages 55–59)

Math Blaster Score	Math Blaster 1	Math Blaster 2	Math Blaster 3	Math Blaster 4	Math Blaster 5	Math Blaster 6	Math Blaster 7	Math Blaster 8	Math Blaster 9	Math Blaster 10
20										
19										
18										
17										
16										
15										
14										
13										
12										
11										
10										
9										
8										
7										
6										
5										
4										
3										
2										
1										

Multiplying by 1 to 12 (pages 60–64)

Math Blaster Score	Math Blaster 1	Math Blaster 2	Math Blaster 3	Math Blaster 4	Math Blaster 5	Math Blaster 6	Math Blaster 7	Math Blaster 8	Math Blaster 9	Math Blaster 10
20										
19										
18										
17										
16										
15										
14										
13										
12										
11										
10										
9										
8										
7										
6										
5										
4										
3										
2										
1										

Multiplication by 10, 100, and 100 (pages 81–85)

Math Blaster Score	Challenge 1	Challenge 2	Challenge 3	Challenge 4	Challenge 5
40					
39					
38					
37					
36					
35					
34					
33					
32					
31					
30					
29					
28					
27					
26					
25					
24					
23					
22					
21					
20					
19					
18					
17					
16					
15					
14					
13					
12					
11					
10					
9					
8					
7					
6					
5					
4					
3					
2					
1					

Multiplication Table for 0 to 12

The numbers on the dark borders are the **factors**.
The numbers inside the table are the **products**.
Try it! To find the product of 6 × 9, for example, find 6 in the left border and put your finger on it.
Then find 9 in the top border and put your finger on it.
Slide your finger on the 6 to the right across the row.
Slide your finger on the 9 down the column. Keep sliding your fingers until they meet.
The number in the square where the row and column meet is the product of the two numbers.
So 6 × 9 = 54.

×	0	1	2	3	4	5	6	7	8	9	10	11	12
0	0	0	0	0	0	0	0	0	0	0	0	0	0
1	0	1	2	3	4	5	6	7	8	9	10	11	12
2	0	2	4	6	8	10	12	14	16	18	20	22	24
3	0	3	6	9	12	15	18	21	24	27	30	33	36
4	0	4	8	12	16	20	24	28	32	36	40	44	48
5	0	5	10	15	20	25	30	35	40	45	50	55	60
6	0	6	12	18	24	30	36	42	48	54	60	66	72
7	0	7	14	21	28	35	42	49	56	63	70	77	84
8	0	8	16	24	32	40	48	56	64	72	80	88	96
9	0	9	18	27	36	45	54	63	72	81	90	99	108
10	0	10	20	30	40	50	60	70	80	90	100	110	120
11	0	11	22	33	44	55	66	77	88	99	110	121	132
12	0	12	24	36	48	60	72	84	96	108	120	132	144

INCREDIBLE WORK!

_____
Name

Answers

Multiply by 0 and 1

The product is always the same as the greater factor when any number is multiplied by 1.

For example, 10 × 1 = 10.

The product is always 0 when any factor is multiplied by 0.

For example, 0 × 4 = 0.

Multiply.

0 × 3 = **0**	2 × 1 = **2**	8 × 1 = **8**	0 × 5 = **0**
3 × 1 = **3**	0 × 8 = **0**	5 × 1 = **5**	7 × 1 = **7**
0 × 12 = **0**	11 × 1 = **11**	0 × 6 = **0**	6 × 1 = **6**
4 × 1 = **4**	0 × 7 = **0**	9 × 1 = **9**	0 × 1 = **0**
0 × 2 = **0**	1 × 1 = **1**	0 × 9 = **0**	12 × 1 = **12**

2

Match Multiplication to Addition: Facts for 2

Complete the multiplication facts for 2. Use a multiplication table to help you. Then write the sums. Underline each matching sum and product. Use a different colour for each pair.

1 × 2 = **2**	2 + 2 + 2 + 2 + 2 = **10**
2 × 2 = **4**	2 + 2 + 2 + 2 + 2 + 2 + 2 + 2 + 2 + 2 + 2 + 2 = **24**
3 × 2 = **6**	2 + 0 = **2**
4 × 2 = **8**	2 + 2 + 2 + 2 + 2 + 2 + 2 + 2 + 2 + 2 = **20**
5 × 2 = **10**	2 + 2 + 2 + 2 + 2 + 2 + 2 = **14**
6 × 2 = **12**	2 + 2 + 2 + 2 + 2 + 2 + 2 + 2 = **16**
7 × 2 = **14**	2 + 2 + 2 = **6**
8 × 2 = **16**	2 + 2 = **4**
9 × 2 = **18**	2 + 2 + 2 + 2 = **8**
10 × 2 = **20**	2 + 2 + 2 + 2 + 2 + 2 + 2 + 2 + 2 = **18**
11 × 2 = **22**	2 + 2 + 2 + 2 + 2 + 2 + 2 + 2 + 2 + 2 + 2 = **22**
12 × 2 = **24**	2 + 2 + 2 + 2 + 2 + 2 = **12**

3

Two Times Table

1. Multiply. Use the key to colour the products.

Colour Key
0 - red
2 - orange
4 - yellow
6 - green
8 - light blue
10 - dark blue
12 - purple
14 - pink
16 - brown
18 - grey
20 - black
22 - gold

7 × 2 = **14**	0 × 2 = **0**	3 × 2 = **6**	8 × 2 = **16**	5 × 2 = **10**
6 × 2 = **12**	2 × 2 = **4**	11 × 2 = **22**	9 × 2 = **18**	4 × 2 = **8**
1 × 2 = **2**	2 × 3 = **6**	12 × 2 = **24**	2 × 7 = **14**	2 × 4 = **8**	2 × 9 = **18**
2 × 10 = **20**	2 × 6 = **12**	2 × 11 = **22**	2 × 0 = **0**	2 × 12 = **24**	2 × 5 = **10**
2 × 8 = **16**	2 × 1 = **2**			

Tip for Multiplying by 2
Double the number!
For example, 4 × 2
Think: 4 + 4 = 8 So 4 × 2 = 8.

Remember to practice skip counting by 2s!

4

Two Times Table (continued)

2. Find the product.

Watch out! Not all of the letters are used in the answer.

A	E	I	M	N
8 × 2 = **16**	5 × 2 = **10**	11 × 2 = **22**	0 × 2 = **0**	12 × 2 = **24**

O	P	S	T	X
1 × 2 = **2**	4 × 2 = **8**	10 × 2 = **20**	2 × 2 = **4**	7 × 2 = **14**

Math Riddle: **What do you call a fake noodle?**

A N   I M P A S T A
16 24   22 0 8 16 20 4 16

3. Find the missing factor.

2 × **6** = 12	**1** × 2 = 2	2 × **9** = 18	**7** × 2 = 14
8 × 2 = 16	2 × **11** = 22	**5** × 2 = 10	2 × **12** = 24
10 × **2** = 20	**4** × 2 = 8	2 × **7** = 14	**3** × 2 = 6
2 × **5** = 10	2 × **10** = 20	**2** × 2 = 4	**0** × 2 = 0

5

Match Multiplication to Addition: Facts for 3

Complete the multiplication facts for 3. Use a multiplication table to help you. Then write the sums. Underline each matching sum and product. Use a different colour for each pair.

1 × 3 = **3**	3 + 3 = **6**
2 × 3 = **6**	3 + 3 + 3 + 3 + 3 + 3 = **18**
3 × 3 = **9**	3 + 3 + 3 + 3 + 3 + 3 + 3 + 3 + 3 + 3 + 3 + 3 = **36**
4 × 3 = **12**	3 + 3 + 3 = **9**
5 × 3 = **15**	3 + 3 + 3 + 3 + 3 + 3 + 3 + 3 + 3 + 3 = **30**
6 × 3 = **18**	3 + 3 + 3 + 3 + 3 + 3 + 3 + 3 = **24**
7 × 3 = **21**	3 + 3 + 3 + 3 + 3 + 3 + 3 + 3 + 3 + 3 + 3 = **33**
8 × 3 = **24**	3 + 3 + 3 + 3 + 3 = **15**
9 × 3 = **27**	3 + 3 + 3 + 3 + 3 + 3 + 3 = **21**
10 × 3 = **30**	3 + 3 + 3 + 3 = **12**
11 × 3 = **33**	3 + 0 = **3**
12 × 3 = **36**	3 + 3 + 3 + 3 + 3 + 3 + 3 + 3 + 3 = **18**

6

Three Times Table

1. Multiply. Use the key to colour the products.

Colour Key
0 - red
3 - orange
6 - yellow
9 - light green
12 - green
15 - light blue
18 - dark blue
21 - purple
24 - pink
27 - brown
30 - grey
33 - black
36 - gold

0 × 3 = **0**	8 × 3 = **24**	9 × 3 = **27**	3 × 3 = **9**	11 × 3 = **33**
5 × 3 = **15**	7 × 3 = **21**	4 × 3 = **12**	2 × 3 = **6**	6 × 3 = **18**
3 × 3 = **9**	3 × 0 = **0**	3 × 2 = **6**	3 × 9 = **27**	3 × 7 = **21**	3 × 4 = **12**
3 × 6 = **18**	3 × 10 = **30**	1 × 3 = **3**	3 × 8 = **24**	3 × 5 = **15**	3 × 1 = **3**
3 × 12 = **36**	3 × 11 = **33**			

Tip for Multiplying by 3
Double the number, and add one more!
For example, 3 × 5.
Think: 2 × 5 = 10. Then add one more 5: 10 + 5 = 15
So 3 × 5 = 15.

Remember to practice skip counting by 3s!

7

Three Times Table (continued)

2. Find the product.

Watch out! Not all of the letters are used in the answer.

E	I	G	O	P
10 × 3 = **30**	7 × 3 = **21**	4 × 3 = **12**	8 × 3 = **24**	2 × 3 = **6**

R	S	T	V	W
6 × 3 = **18**	12 × 3 = **36**	9 × 3 = **27**	5 × 3 = **15**	3 × 3 = **9**

Math Riddle: **Why was the broom late?**

I T   O V E R S W E P T
21 27   24 15 30 18 36 9 30 6 27

3. Find the missing factor.

3 × **4** = 12	**1** × 3 = 3	3 × **2** = 6	**0** × 3 = 0
8 × 3 = 24	3 × **9** = 27	**7** × 3 = 21	3 × **5** = 15
10 × **3** = 30	**11** × 3 = 33	3 × **3** = 9	3 × **8** = 24
5 × 3 = 15	3 × **12** = 36	**10** × 3 = 30	**6** × 3 = 18

8

Multiply by 1, 2, and 3

1. Find the product. Colour odd products red. Colour even products blue.

9 × 1 = **9**	1 × 2 = **2**	9 × 3 = **27**	4 × 2 = **8**	4 × 1 = **4**
3 × 2 = **6**	5 × 3 = **15**	1 × 1 = **1**	7 × 2 = **14**	6 × 3 = **18**
5 × 2 = **10**	2 × 1 = **2**	0 × 3 = **0**	2 × 3 = **6**	3 × 1 = **3**
0 × 2 = **0**	5 × 1 = **5**	2 × 2 = **4**	6 × 1 = **6**	8 × 2 = **16**
3 × 3 = **9**	9 × 2 = **18**	7 × 3 = **21**	6 × 2 = **12**	8 × 3 = **24**
0 × 1 = **0**	4 × 3 = **12**	7 × 1 = **7**	1 × 3 = **3**	8 × 1 = **8**

9

© Chalkboard Publishing

91

Page 10 — Math Riddle: Multiplication Facts for 1, 2, and 3

Why did the rocketship go to the doctor?

I T | N E E D E D | T O | G E T
7 10 | 9 9 4 9 4 | 10 30 | 5 9 10

A | B O O S T E R | S H O T
3 | 24 30 30 15 10 9 22 | 15 36 30 10

A: 3 ×1 = **3**	B: 12 ×2 = **24**	C: 8 ×2 = **16**	D: 2 ×2 = **4**	E: 9 ×1 = **9**
G: 5 ×1 = **5**	H: 12 ×3 = **36**	I: 7 ×1 = **7**	N: 3 ×2 = **6**	O: 10 ×3 = **30**
P: 6 ×3 = **18**	Q: 1 ×1 = **1**	R: 11 ×2 = **22**	S: 5 ×3 = **15**	T: 5 ×2 = **10**

Watch out! Not all of the letters are used in the answer.

Page 11 — Match Multiplication to Addition: Facts for 4

Complete the multiplication facts for 4. Use a multiplication table to help you. Then write the sums. Underline each matching sum and product. Use a different colour for each pair.

1 × 4 = **4**	4 + 4 + 4 + 4 + 4 = **20**
2 × 4 = **8**	4 + 4 + 4 + 4 + 4 + 4 + 4 + 4 + 4 + 4 + 4 + 4 = **48**
3 × 4 = **12**	4 + 4 + 4 + 4 + 4 + 4 + 4 = **28**
4 × 4 = **16**	4 + 4 + 4 + 4 + 4 + 4 + 4 + 4 + 4 + 4 = **40**
5 × 4 = **20**	4 + 4 = **16**
6 × 4 = **24**	4 + 0 = **0**
7 × 4 = **28**	4 + 4 + 4 + 4 + 4 + 4 = **24**
8 × 4 = **32**	4 + 4 + 4 + 4 + 4 + 4 + 4 + 4 + 4 + 4 + 4 = **44**
9 × 4 = **36**	4 + 4 + 4 + 4 + 4 = **40**
10 × 4 = **40**	4 + 4 + 4 + 4 + 4 + 4 + 4 + 4 = **32**
11 × 4 = **44**	4 + 4 + 4 + 4 + 4 + 4 + 4 + 4 + 4 = **36**
12 × 4 = **48**	4 + 4 + 4 = **12**

Page 12 — Four Times Table

1. Multiply. Use the key to colour the products.

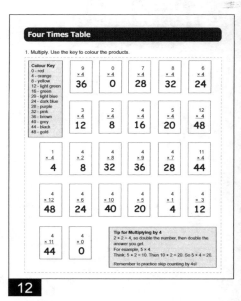

Colour Key
0 - red, 4 - orange, 8 - yellow, 12 - light green, 16 - green, 20 - light blue, 24 - dark blue, 28 - purple, 32 - pink, 36 - brown, 40 - grey, 44 - black, 48 - gold

9 ×4 = **36**	0 ×4 = **0**	7 ×4 = **28**	8 ×4 = **32**	6 ×4 = **24**
3 ×4 = **12**	4 ×2 = **8**	4 ×4 = **16**	5 ×4 = **20**	12 ×4 = **48**
1 ×4 = **4**	4 ×2 = **8**	4 ×8 = **32**	4 ×9 = **36**	4 ×7 = **28** / 11 ×4 = **44**
4 ×12 = **48**	4 ×6 = **24**	4 ×10 = **40**	4 ×5 = **20**	4 ×1 = **4** / 4 ×3 = **12**
4 ×11 = **44**	4 ×0 = **0**			

Tip for Multiplying by 4
2 × 2 = 4, so double the number, then double the answer you get.
For example, 5 × 4
Think: 5 × 2 = 10. Then 10 × 2 = 20. So 5 × 4 = 20.
Remember to practice skip counting by 4s!

Page 13 — Four Times Table (continued)

Watch out! Not all of the letters are used in the answer.

2. Find the product.

| A: 0 × 4 = **0** | B: 3 × 4 = **12** | C: 8 × 4 = **32** | E: 2 × 4 = **8** | G: 12 × 4 = **48** |
| L: 9 × 4 = **36** | U: 5 × 4 = **20** | K: 11 × 4 = **44** | R: 6 × 4 = **24** | T: 7 × 4 = **28** |

Math Riddle: What vehicle has four wheels and flies?

A G A R B A G E   T R U C K
0   48 0 24 12 0 48 8   28 24 20 32 44

3. Find the missing factor.

3 × **4** = 12	**2** × 4 = 8	4 × **6** = 24	**8** × 4 = 32
4 × 4 = 16	4 × **7** = 28	**9** × 4 = 36	4 × **11** = 44
10 × **4** = 40	**2** × 4 = 8	4 × **12** = 48	**6** × 4 = 24
4 × 9 = 36	4 × **5** = 20	**1** × 4 = 4	**0** × 4 = 0

Page 14 — Match Multiplication to Addition: Facts for 5

Complete the multiplication facts for 5. Use a multiplication table to help you. Then write the sums. Underline each matching sum and product. Use a different colour for each pair.

1 × 5 = **5**	5 + 5 + 5 + 5 = **20**
2 × 5 = **10**	5 + 5 + 5 + 5 + 5 = **25**
3 × 5 = **15**	5 + 5 + 5 + 5 + 5 + 5 + 5 + 5 + 5 + 5 + 5 = **55**
4 × 5 = **20**	5 + 5 + 5 + 5 + 5 + 5 + 5 + 5 + 5 = **45**
5 × 5 = **25**	5 + 5 + 5 + 5 + 5 + 5 + 5 + 5 + 5 + 5 + 5 + 5 = **60**
6 × 5 = **30**	5 + 0 = **5**
7 × 5 = **35**	5 + 5 + 5 + 5 + 5 + 5 + 5 + 5 + 5 + 5 = **50**
8 × 5 = **40**	5 + 5 + 5 = **15**
9 × 5 = **45**	5 + 5 = **10**
10 × 5 = **50**	5 + 5 + 5 + 5 + 5 + 5 = **30**
11 × 5 = **55**	5 + 5 + 5 + 5 + 5 + 5 + 5 = **35**
12 × 5 = **60**	5 + 5 + 5 + 5 + 5 + 5 + 5 + 5 = **40**

Page 15 — Five Times Table

1. Multiply. Use the key to colour the products.

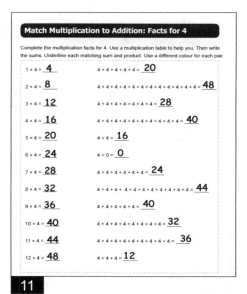

Colour Key
0 - red, 5 - orange, 10 - yellow, 15 - light green, 20 - green, 25 - light blue, 30 - dark blue, 35 - purple, 40 - pink, 45 - brown, 50 - grey, 55 - black, 60 - gold

6 ×5 = **30**	0 ×5 = **0**	7 ×5 = **35**	9 ×5 = **45**	8 ×5 = **40**
1 ×5 = **5**	2 ×5 = **10**	11 ×5 = **55**	3 ×5 = **15**	4 ×5 = **20**
5 ×5 = **25**	12 ×5 = **60**	5 ×2 = **10**	5 ×0 = **0**	5 ×9 = **45** / 5 ×4 = **20**
5 ×11 = **55**	5 ×6 = **30**	5 ×3 = **15**	5 ×8 = **40**	5 ×1 = **5** / 5 ×12 = **60**
5 ×10 = **50**	5 ×7 = **35**			

Tip for Multiplying by 5
The answer always ends in 5 or 0.
The product is half the number times 10.
For example, for 5 × 6, half of 6 is 3.
10 × 3 = 30. So 5 × 6 = 30.
Remember to practice skip counting by 5s!

Page 16 — Five Times Table (continued)

Watch out! Not all of the letters are used in the answer.

2. Find the product.

| A: 7 × 5 = **35** | E: 9 × 5 = **45** | F: 1 × 5 = **5** | H: 4 × 5 = **20** | L: 12 × 5 = **60** |
| M: 6 × 5 = **30** | O: 3 × 5 = **15** | P: 8 × 5 = **40** | S: 10 × 5 = **50** | T: 5 × 5 = **25** |

Math Riddle: How many months of the year have 28 days?

A L L   O F   T H E M
35 60 60   15 5   25 20 45 30

3. Find the missing factor.

3 × **5** = 15	**4** × 5 = 20	5 × **11** = 55	**2** × 5 = 10
9 × 5 = 45	**0** × 5 = 0	**8** × 5 = 40	5 × **6** = 30
1 × **5** = 5	**7** × 5 = 35	5 × **1** = 5	**5** × 5 = 25
3 × 5 = 15	2 × **5** = 10	**5** × 12 = 60	10 × **5** = 50

Page 17 — Match Multiplication to Addition: Facts for 6

Complete the multiplication facts for 6. Use a multiplication table to help you. Then write the sums. Underline each matching sum and product. Use a different colour for each pair.

1 × 6 = **6**	6 + 6 + 6 + 6 + 6 + 6 = **36**
2 × 6 = **12**	6 + 6 + 6 + 6 + 6 + 6 + 6 + 6 + 6 + 6 + 6 = **66**
3 × 6 = **18**	6 + 6 + 6 + 6 + 6 + 6 + 6 + 6 + 6 = **54**
4 × 6 = **24**	6 + 6 + 6 + 6 + 6 + 6 + 6 = **42**
5 × 6 = **30**	6 + 6 = **12**
6 × 6 = **36**	6 + 6 + 6 + 6 + 6 + 6 + 6 + 6 + 6 + 6 + 6 + 6 = **72**
7 × 6 = **42**	6 + 6 + 6 + 6 = **24**
8 × 6 = **48**	6 + 0 = **6**
9 × 6 = **54**	6 + 6 + 6 = **18**
10 × 6 = **60**	6 + 6 + 6 + 6 + 6 + 6 + 6 + 6 = **48**
11 × 6 = **66**	6 + 6 + 6 + 6 + 6 = **30**
12 × 6 = **72**	6 + 6 + 6 + 6 + 6 + 6 + 6 + 6 + 6 + 6 = **60**

Page 18 — Six Times Table

1. Multiply. Use the key to colour the products.

Colour Key
0 - red, 6 - orange, 12 - yellow, 18 - light green, 24 - green, 30 - light blue, 36 - dark blue, 42 - purple, 48 - pink, 54 - brown, 60 - grey, 66 - black, 72 - gold

2 ×6 = **12**	0 ×6 = **0**	9 ×6 = **54**	3 ×6 = **18**	1 ×6 = **6**
7 ×6 = **42**	8 ×6 = **48**	4 ×6 = **24**	5 ×6 = **30**	6 ×6 = **36**
6 ×12 = **72**	11 ×6 = **66**	6 ×2 = **12**	6 ×0 = **0**	6 ×9 = **54** / 6 ×4 = **24**
6 ×10 = **60**	6 ×7 = **42**	6 ×1 = **6**	6 ×5 = **30**	12 ×6 = **72** / 6 ×3 = **18**
6 ×11 = **66**	6 ×8 = **48**			

Tip for Multiplying by 6
When multiplying 6 by an even number, the answer always ends in the same number you multiplied 6 by.
For example, 6 × 2 = 12.
In the answer, the tens column is always half the ones column. For example, 6 × 6 = 36.
Remember to practice skip counting by 6s!

92

Six Times Table (continued)

2. Find the product.

A	B	E	H	I
3 × 6 = **18**	11 × 6 = **66**	8 × 6 = **48**	9 × 6 = **54**	5 × 6 = **30**

K	N	R	T	V
2 × 6 = **12**	10 × 6 = **60**	6 × 6 = **36**	12 × 6 = **72**	4 × 6 = **24**

Math Riddle: **Where do some fish keep their money?**

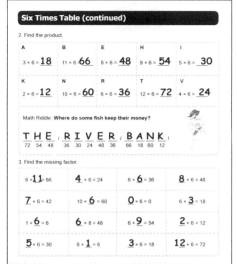

T H E   R I V E R   B A N K
72 54 48   36 30 24 48 36   66 18 60 12

3. Find the missing factor.

6 × **11** = 66	**4** × 6 = 24	6 × **6** = 36	**8** × 6 = 48
7 × 6 = 42	10 × **6** = 60	**0** × 6 = 0	6 × **3** = 18
1 × **6** = 6	**6** × 8 = 48	6 × **9** = 54	**2** × 6 = 12
5 × 6 = 30	6 × **1** = 6	**3** × 6 = 18	**12** × 6 = 72

19

Multiply by 4, 5, and 6

1. Find the product. Colour odd products red. Colour even products blue.

9 × 4 = **36**	11 × 6 = **66**	9 × 5 = **45**	4 × 6 = **24**	4 × 4 = **16**
3 × 6 = **18**	3 × 5 = **15**	11 × 4 = **44**	7 × 6 = **42**	3 × 6 = **18**
5 × 6 = **30**	2 × 4 = **8**	12 × 5 = **60**	10 × 5 = **50**	3 × 4 = **12**
12 × 6 = **72**	5 × 4 = **20**	2 × 6 = **12**	4 × 6 = **24**	8 × 6 = **48**
3 × 5 = **15**	9 × 6 = **54**	7 × 5 = **35**	6 × 6 = **36**	8 × 5 = **40**
12 × 4 = **48**	5 × 4 = **20**	7 × 4 = **28**	11 × 5 = **55**	8 × 4 = **32**

20

Math Riddle: Multiplication Facts for 4, 5, and 6

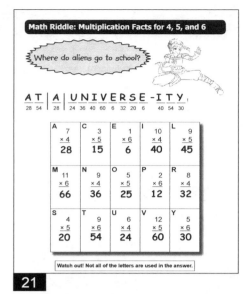

Where do aliens go to school?

A T   A   U N I V E R S E - I T Y
28 54   28   24 36 40 60 6 32 20 6   40 54 30

A 7 ×4 = **28**	C 3 ×5 = **15**	E 1 ×6 = **6**	I 10 ×4 = **40**	L 9 ×5 = **45**
M 11 ×6 = **66**	N 9 ×4 = **36**	O 5 ×5 = **25**	P 2 ×6 = **12**	R 8 ×4 = **32**
S 4 ×5 = **20**	T 9 ×6 = **54**	U 6 ×4 = **24**	V 12 ×5 = **60**	Y 5 ×6 = **30**

Watch out! Not all of the letters are used in the answer.

21

Match Multiplication to Addition: Facts for 7

Complete the multiplication facts for 7. Use a multiplication table to help you. Then write the sums. Underline each matching sum and product. Use a different colour for each pair.

1 × 7 = **7**	7 + 7 + 7 + 7 + 7 + 7 + 7 + 7 + 7 + 7 + 7 + 7 = **84**
2 × 7 = **14**	7 + 7 + 7 + 7 + 7 + 7 + 7 + 7 + 7 = **63**
3 × 7 = **21**	7 + 7 + 7 + 7 + 7 = **35**
4 × 7 = **28**	7 + 7 + 7 + 7 + 7 + 7 = **42**
5 × 7 = **35**	7 + 7 = **14**
6 × 7 = **42**	7 + 7 + 7 + 7 + 7 + 7 + 7 + 7 + 7 + 7 = **70**
7 × 7 = **49**	7 + 7 + 7 + 7 = **28**
8 × 7 = **56**	7 + 7 + 7 + 7 + 7 + 7 + 7 + 7 + 7 + 7 + 7 = **77**
9 × 7 = **63**	7 + 7 + 7 = **21**
10 × 7 = **70**	7 + 7 + 7 + 7 + 7 + 7 + 7 = **49**
11 × 7 = **77**	7 + 0 = **7**
12 × 7 = **84**	7 + 7 + 7 + 7 + 7 + 7 + 7 + 7 = **56**

22

Seven Times Table

1. Multiply. Use the key to colour the products.

Colour Key
0 - red
14 - yellow
21 - light green
28 - green
35 - light blue
42 - dark blue
49 - purple
56 - pink
63 - brown
70 - grey
77 - black
84 - gold

3 ×7 = **21**	0 ×7 = **0**	8 ×7 = **56**	6 ×7 = **42**	11 ×7 = **77**
12 ×7 = **84**	7 ×7 = **49**	4 ×7 = **28**	2 ×7 = **14**	9 ×7 = **63**
5 ×7 = **35**	2 ×7 = **14**	8 ×7 = **56**	1 ×7 = **7**	12 ×7 = **84**	4 ×7 = **28**
7 ×11 = **77**	5 ×7 = **35**	3 ×7 = **21**	7 ×6 = **42**	9 ×7 = **63**	7 ×1 = **7**
7 ×0 = **0**	7 ×10 = **70**			

Tip for Multiplying by 7
Multiply 7 by a number that you know close to the number. For 7 × 7 =, you know 5 × 7 = 35. Then 7 − 5 = 2 more 7s. Multiply the remaining 7s and add them to your answer. Think: 5 × 7 = 35, and 2 × 7 = 14.
35 + 14 = 49. So 7 × 7 = 49.

Remember to practice skip counting by 7s!

23

Seven Times Table (continued)

2. Find the product.

Watch out! Not all of the letters are used in the answer.

A	C	D	E	H
5 × 7 = **35**	7 × 7 = **49**	3 × 7 = **21**	10 × 7 = **70**	8 × 7 = **56**

L	M	N	P	S
12 × 7 = **84**	4 × 7 = **28**	6 × 7 = **42**	9 × 7 = **63**	11 × 7 = **77**

Math Riddle: **What kind of dog loves to have baths?**

A   S H A M P O O D L E
35   77 56 35 28 63 21 84 70

3. Find the missing factor.

2 × **7** = 14	**1** × 7 = 7	3 × **7** = 21	**8** × 7 = 56
10 × 7 = 70	12 × **7** = 84	**7** × 6 = 42	7 × **7** = 49
7 × **8** = 56	**5** × 7 = 35	7 × **10** = 70	**0** × 7 = 0
11 × 7 = 77	7 × **2** = 14	9 × **7** = 63	**4** × 7 = 28

24

Match Multiplication to Addition: Facts for 8

Complete the multiplication facts for 8. Use a multiplication table to help you. Then write the sums. Underline each matching sum and product. Use a different colour for each pair.

1 × 8 = **8**	8 + 8 + 8 + 8 + 8 + 8 + 8 + 8 + 8 + 8 + 8 = **88**
2 × 8 = **16**	8 + 8 + 8 + 8 + 8 + 8 = **48**
3 × 8 = **24**	8 + 8 + 8 + 8 + 8 + 8 + 8 + 8 + 8 + 8 = **80**
4 × 8 = **32**	8 + 8 = **16**
5 × 8 = **40**	8 + 8 + 8 + 8 + 8 + 8 + 8 + 8 + 8 + 8 + 8 + 8 = **96**
6 × 8 = **48**	8 + 8 + 8 + 8 + 8 + 8 + 8 + 8 = **64**
7 × 8 = **56**	8 + 8 + 8 = **24**
8 × 8 = **64**	8 + 8 + 8 + 8 + 8 = **40**
9 × 8 = **72**	8 + 0 = **8**
10 × 8 = **80**	8 + 8 + 8 + 8 = **32**
11 × 8 = **88**	8 + 8 + 8 + 8 + 8 + 8 + 8 = **56**
12 × 8 = **96**	8 + 8 + 8 + 8 + 8 + 8 + 8 + 8 = **63**

25

Eight Times Table

1. Multiply. Use the key to colour the products.

Colour Key
0 - red
8 - orange
16 - yellow
24 - light green
32 - green
40 - light blue
48 - dark blue
56 - purple
64 - pink
72 - brown
80 - grey
88 - black
96 - gold

3 ×8 = **24**	9 ×8 = **72**	8 ×8 = **64**	0 ×8 = **0**	11 ×8 = **88**
5 ×8 = **40**	7 ×8 = **56**	4 ×8 = **32**	2 ×8 = **16**	6 ×8 = **48**
1 ×8 = **8**	12 ×8 = **96**	8 ×2 = **16**	8 ×5 = **40**	8 ×9 = **72**	8 ×4 = **32**
8 ×11 = **88**	8 ×6 = **48**	8 ×3 = **24**	8 ×7 = **56**	8 ×12 = **96**	8 ×1 = **8**
8 ×10 = **80**	8 ×0 = **0**			

Tip for Multiplying by 8
Doubling 4 gives you 8, so double the number you multiply by 4 to get the multiple for 8!
For 8 × 8 =, you know that 4 × 8 = 32.
Next, double the 32. 32 × 2 = 64. So 8 × 8 = 64.

Remember to practice skip counting by 8s!

26

Eight Times Table (continued)

2. Find the product.

Watch out! Not all of the letters are used in the answer.

A	C	E	H	M
8 × 8 = **64**	2 × 8 = **16**	12 × 8 = **96**	9 × 8 = **72**	0 × 8 = **0**

P	R	S	T	W
4 × 8 = **32**	10 × 8 = **80**	5 × 8 = **40**	6 × 8 = **48**	7 × 8 = **56**

Math Riddle: **What do cats like to read in the morning?**

T H E   M E W S P A P E R
48 72 96   0 96 56 40 32 64 32 96 80

3. Find the missing factor.

4 × **8** = 32	**7** × 8 = 56	2 × **8** = 16	**12** × 8 = 96
5 × 8 = 40	8 × **4** = 32	**1** × 8 = 8	10 × **8** = 80
12 × **8** = 96	**3** × 8 = 24	8 × **9** = 72	**11** × 8 = 88
6 × 8 = 48	3 × **8** = 24	**8** × 8 = 64	**0** × 8 = 0

27

Match Multiplication to Addition: Facts for 9

Complete the multiplication facts for 9. Use a multiplication table to help you. Then write the sums. Underline each matching sum and product. Use a different colour for each pair.

1 × 9 = **9**	9 + 9 + 9 + 9 + 9 + 9 + 9 + 9 + 9 + 9 + 9 + 9 = **108**
2 × 9 = **18**	9 + 9 + 9 + 9 + 9 + 9 + 9 = **63**
3 × 9 = **27**	9 + 9 + 9 + 9 + 9 + 9 + 9 + 9 + 9 + 9 + 9 = **99**
4 × 9 = **36**	9 + 9 + 9 + 9 + 9 + 9 = **54**
5 × 9 = **45**	9 + 0 = **9**
6 × 9 = **54**	9 + 9 + 9 + 9 = **36**
7 × 9 = **63**	9 + 9 = **18**
8 × 9 = **72**	9 + 9 + 9 + 9 + 9 + 9 + 9 + 9 + 9 + 9 = **90**
9 × 9 = **81**	9 + 9 + 9 + 9 + 9 + 9 + 9 + 9 + 9 = **81**
10 × 9 = **90**	9 + 9 + 9 + 9 + 9 + 9 + 9 + 9 = **72**
11 × 9 = **99**	9 + 9 + 9 + 9 + 9 = **45**
12 × 9 = **108**	9 + 9 + 9 = **27**

28

Nine Times Table

1. Multiply. Use the key to colour the products.

Colour Key
0 - red
9 - orange
18 - yellow
27 - light green
36 - green
45 - dark blue
54 - dark blue
63 - purple
72 - pink
81 - brown
90 - grey
99 - black
108 - gold

7 × 9 = **63**	6 × 9 = **54**	3 × 9 = **27**	1 × 9 = **9**	0 × 9 = **0**
5 × 9 = **45**	2 × 9 = **18**	4 × 9 = **36**	8 × 9 = **72**	12 × 9 = **108**
9 × 9 = **81**	9 × 6 = **54**	9 × 2 = **18**	9 × 7 = **63**	11 × 9 = **99**	9 × 4 = **36**
9 × 1 = **9**	9 × 8 = **72**	9 × 3 = **27**	9 × 5 = **45**	9 × 12 = **108**	9 × 10 = **90**
9 × 0 = **0**	9 × 11 = **99**				

Tip for Multiplying by 9
Multiply the number by 10, then subtract one of that number from the answer. For example,
7 × 9 =
Think: 7 × 10 = 70. 70 − 7 = 63. So 7 × 9 = 63.
Remember to practice skip counting by 9s!

29

Nine Times Table (continued)

2. Find the product.

A	E	G	I	L
12 × 9 = **108**	6 × 9 = **54**	11 × 9 = **99**	8 × 9 = **72**	0 × 9 = **0**

N	P	S	T	W
10 × 9 = **90**	1 × 9 = **9**	7 × 9 = **63**	5 × 9 = **45**	4 × 9 = **36**

Math Riddle: **Why did the banana go to the doctor?**

I T   W A S N T   P E E L I N G
72 45   36 108 63 90 45   9   54 54   0   72 90 99

W E L L !
36 54   0 0

3. Find the missing factor.

9 × **2** = 18	9 × **5** = 45	11 × **9** = 99	**9** × 9 = 81
0 × 9 = 0	**4** × 9 = 36	**6** × 9 = 54	9 × **3** = 27
10 × **9** = 90	**12** × 9 = 108	9 × **1** = 9	**5** × 9 = 45
9 × **11** = 99	**8** × 9 = 72	**7** × 9 = 63	2 × **9** = 18

30

Multiply by 7, 8, and 9

1. Find the product. Colour odd products red. Colour even products blue.

9 × 7 = **63**	11 × 9 = **99**	9 × 8 = **72**	4 × 9 = **36**	4 × 7 = **28**
3 × 9 = **27**	5 × 8 = **40**	11 × 7 = **77**	7 × 9 = **63**	6 × 8 = **48**
5 × 9 = **45**	2 × 7 = **14**	12 × 8 = **96**	10 × 8 = **80**	3 × 7 = **21**
12 × 9 = **108**	5 × 7 = **35**	2 × 9 = **18**	6 × 7 = **42**	8 × 9 = **72**
3 × 8 = **24**	9 × 9 = **81**	7 × 8 = **56**	6 × 9 = **54**	8 × 8 = **64**
12 × 7 = **84**	4 × 8 = **32**	7 × 7 = **49**	11 × 8 = **88**	10 × 7 = **70**

31

Math Riddle: Multiplication Facts for 7, 8, and 9

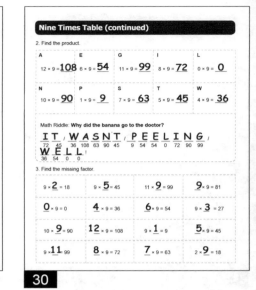

How do aliens stay clean?

T H E Y   T A K E
77 42 27 54   77 84   9 27

M E T E O R   S H O W E R S
88 27 77 27 63 72   108 42   63 40 27 72 108

	A	D	E	H	I
	12 × 7 = **84**	8 × 8 = **64**	3 × 9 = **27**	6 × 7 = **42**	2 × 8 = **16**
	K	L	M	O	P
	1 × 9 = **9**	3 × 7 = **21**	11 × 8 = **88**	7 × 9 = **63**	10 × 7 = **70**
	R	S	T	W	Y
	9 × 8 = **72**	12 × 9 = **108**	11 × 7 = **77**	5 × 8 = **40**	6 × 9 = **54**

Watch out! Not all of the letters are used in the answer.

32

Match Multiplication to Addition: Facts for 10

Complete the multiplication facts for 10. Use a multiplication table to help you. Then write the sums. Underline each matching sum and product. Use a different colour for each pair.

1 × 10 = **10**	10 + 10 + 10 + 10 + 10 = **50**
2 × 10 = **20**	10 + 10 + 10 + 10 = **40**
3 × 10 = **30**	10 + 10 + 10 + 10 + 10 + 10 + 10 + 10 = **80**
4 × 10 = **40**	10 + 10 + 10 + 10 + 10 + 10 + 10 = **70**
5 × 10 = **50**	10 + 10 + 10 + 10 + 10 + 10 + 10 + 10 + 10 + 10 = **100**
6 × 10 = **60**	10 + 10 + 10 = **30**
7 × 10 = **70**	10 + 0 = **10**
8 × 10 = **80**	10 + 10 + 10 + 10 + 10 + 10 + 10 + 10 + 10 = **90**
9 × 10 = **90**	10 + 10 + 10 + 10 + 10 + 10 + 10 + 10 + 10 + 10 + 10 + 10 = **120**
10 × 10 = **100**	10 + 10 + 10 + 10 + 10 + 10 + 10 + 10 + 10 + 10 + 10 = **110**
11 × 10 = **110**	10 + 10 = **20**
12 × 10 = **120**	10 + 10 + 10 + 10 + 10 + 10 = **60**

33

Ten Times Table

1. Multiply. Use the key to colour the products.

Colour Key
0 - red
10 - orange
20 - yellow
30 - light green
40 - green
50 - dark blue
60 - dark blue
70 - purple
80 - pink
90 - brown
100 - grey
110 - black
120 - gold

9 × 10 = **90**	6 × 10 = **60**	3 × 10 = **30**	8 × 10 = **80**	0 × 10 = **0**
4 × 10 = **40**	2 × 10 = **20**	5 × 10 = **50**	7 × 10 = **70**	11 × 10 = **110**
10 × 3 = **30**	10 × 8 = **80**	10 × 10 = **100**	10 × 6 = **60**	10 × 9 = **90**	10 × 1 = **10**
10 × 11 = **110**	10 × 2 = **20**	10 × 7 = **70**	10 × 5 = **50**	10 × 12 = **120**	10 × 4 = **40**
10 × 10 = **100**	10 × 0 = **0**				

Tip for Multiplying by 10
When multiplying by 10, just add 0!
For example, 6 × 10 = 60.

Remember to practice skip counting by 10s!

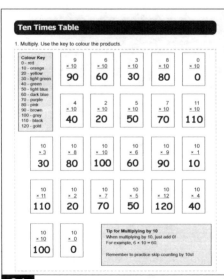

34

Ten Times Table (continued)

2. Find the product.

E	F	G	H	I
12 × 10 = **120**	4 × 10 = **40**	5 × 10 = **50**	10 × 10 = **100**	0 × 10 = **0**

K	R	S	T	Y
11 × 10 = **110**	1 × 10 = **10**	6 × 10 = **60**	9 × 10 = **90**	3 × 10 = **30**

Math Riddle: **Why was the piano locked out?**

I T   F O R G O T   T H E   K E Y
0 90   40 60 10 50 60 90   90 100 120   110 120 30

3. Find the missing factor.

2 × **10** = 20	**6** × 10 = 60	10 × **11** = 110	**5** × 10 = 50
10 × 2 = 20	10 × **7** = 70	**0** × 10 = 0	10 × **1** = 10
10 × **9** = 90	**8** × 10 = 80	5 × **10** = 50	**10** × 10 = 100
4 × 10 = 40	10 × **11** = 110	**10** × 12 = 120	3 × **10** = 30

35

Math Riddle: Multiplication Facts from 1 to 10

Where does an alien park its spaceship?

A T   A   P A R K I N G
40 96   40   40 48 40 18 25 44 14   3

M E T E O R
24 63 96 63 120 18

A	C	E	G	I	K
10 × 4 = **40**	3 × 5 = **15**	7 × 9 = **63**	1 × 3 = **3**	11 × 4 = **44**	5 × 5 = **25**
L	M	N	O	P	R
8 × 1 = **8**	4 × 6 = **24**	2 × 7 = **14**	12 × 10 = **120**	6 × 8 = **48**	9 × 2 = **18**
S	T				
5 × 10 = **50**	12 × 8 = **96**				

Watch out! Not all of the letters are used in the answer.

36

Match Multiplication to Addition: Facts for 11 — 37

Complete the multiplication facts for 11. Use a multiplication table to help you. Then write the sums. Underline each matching sum and product. Use a different colour for each pair.

1 × 11 = **11**   11 + 11 + 11 + 11 + 11 + 11 + 11 + 11 + 11 = **99**
2 × 11 = **22**   11 + 11 + 11 + 11 + 11 + 11 + 11 = **77**
3 × 11 = **33**   11 + 11 + 11 + 11 + 11 + 11 + 11 + 11 + 11 + 11 + 11 + 11 = **132**
4 × 11 = **44**   11 + 11 + 11 + 11 + 11 + 11 + 11 + 11 + 11 + 11 + 11 = **121**
5 × 11 = **55**   11 + 11 + 11 + 11 + 11 = **55**
6 × 11 = **66**   11 + 11 + 11 + 11 + 11 + 11 + 11 + 11 = **88**
7 × 11 = **77**   11 + 11 + 11 + 11 + 11 + 11 + 11 + 11 + 11 + 11 = **110**
8 × 11 = **88**   11 + 11 + 11 = **33**
9 × 11 = **99**   11 + 0 = **11**
10 × 11 = **110**   11 + 11 + 11 + 11 = **44**
11 × 11 = **121**   11 + 11 + 11 + 11 + 11 + 11 = **66**
12 × 11 = **132**   11 + 11 = **22**

Eleven Times Table — 38

1. Multiply. Use the key to colour the products.

Colour Key
0 - red
11 - orange
22 - yellow
33 - light green
44 - green
55 - light blue
66 - dark blue
77 - purple
88 - pink
99 - brown
110 - grey
121 - black
132 - gold

0 ×11 = **0**	8 ×11 = **88**	3 ×11 = **33**	9 ×11 = **99**	6 ×11 = **66**
2 ×11 = **22**	4 ×11 = **44**	5 ×11 = **55**	7 ×11 = **77**	1 ×11 = **11**
11 ×8 = **88**	12 = **132**	11 = **22**	11 ×9 = **77**	11 ×9 = **99**	11 ×4 = **44**
11 = **121**	11 ×6 = **66**	11 = **55**	11 ×3 = **33**	11 = **132**	11 ×0 = **0**
11 ×10 = **110**	11 ×1 = **11**

Tip for Multiplying by 11
When multiplying a number up to 9 × 11, just write the digit twice!
For example, 5 × 11 = 55.

Remember to practice skip counting by 11s!

Eleven Times Table (continued) — 39

Watch out! Not all of the letters are used in the answer.

2. Find the product.

A   11 × 11 = **121**
E   7 × 11 = **77**
I   0 × 11 = **0**
L   9 × 11 = **99**
M   4 × 11 = **44**

P   12 × 11 = **132**
Q   8 × 11 = **88**
S   5 × 11 = **55**
T   3 × 11 = **33**
U   6 × 11 = **66**

Math Riddle: What vegetables do librarians like the most?

Q U I E T   P E A S
88 66 0 77 33   132 77 121 55

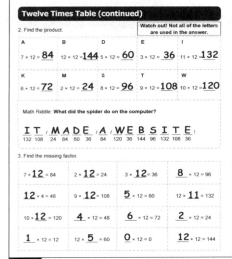

3. Find the missing factor.

11 × **3** = 33   **6** × 11 = 66   5 × **11** = 55   **4** × 11 = 44
11 × 6 = 66   11 × **11** = 121   **11** × 1 = 11   11 × **7** = 77
10 × **11** = 110   **11** × 2 = 22   11 × **8** = 88   **5** × 11 = 55
121 × 1 = 132   11 × **1** = 11   **9** × 11 = 99   **0** × 11 = 0

Match Multiplication to Addition: Facts for 12 — 40

Complete the multiplication facts for 12. Use a multiplication table to help you. Then write the sums. Underline each matching sum and product. Use a different colour for each pair.

1 × 12 = **12**   12 + 12 + 12 + 12 + 12 + 12 + 12 + 12 = **96**
2 × 12 = **24**   12 + 12 + 12 + 12 + 12 + 12 + 12 = **84**
3 × 12 = **36**   12 + 12 + 12 + 12 + 12 = **60**
4 × 12 = **48**   12 + 12 + 12 + 12 + 12 + 12 + 12 + 12 + 12 + 12 = **120**
5 × 12 = **60**   12 + 12 + 12 + 12 + 12 + 12 + 12 + 12 + 12 + 12 + 12 + 12 = **144**
6 × 12 = **72**   12 + 12 + 12 = **36**
7 × 12 = **84**   12 + 12 = **24**
8 × 12 = **96**   12 + 12 + 12 + 12 + 12 + 12 + 12 + 12 + 12 = **108**
9 × 12 = **108**   12 + 12 + 12 + 12 = **48**
10 × 12 = **120**   12 + 0 = **12**
11 × 12 = **132**   12 + 12 + 12 + 12 + 12 + 12 = **72**
12 × 12 = **144**   12 + 12 + 12 + 12 + 12 + 12 + 12 + 12 + 12 + 12 + 12 = **132**

Twelve Times Table — 41

1. Multiply. Use the key to colour the products.

Colour Key
0 - red
12 - orange
24 - yellow
36 - light green
48 - green
60 - light blue
72 - dark blue
84 - purple
96 - pink
108 - brown
120 - grey
132 - black
144 - gold

3 ×12 = **36**	0 ×12 = **0**	8 ×12 = **96**	9 ×12 = **108**	11 ×12 = **132**
5 ×12 = **60**	1 ×12 = **12**	2 ×12 = **24**	7 ×12 = **84**	6 ×12 = **72**
12 ×10 = **120**	12 ×8 = **96**	12 ×2 = **24**	12 ×4 = **48**	12 ×9 = **108**	12 ×11 = **132**
12 ×3 = **36**	12 ×6 = **72**	4 ×12 = **48**	12 ×12 = **144**	12 ×5 = **60**	12 ×7 = **84**
12 ×1 = **12**	12 ×0 = **0**

Tip for Multiplying by 12
Remember that every fact has a twin.
So 3 × 12 has a twin called 12 × 3.
If you know the fact for 3, multiplying becomes easy!

Remember to practice skip counting by 12s!

Twelve Times Table (continued) — 42

Watch out! Not all of the letters are used in the answer.

2. Find the product.

A   7 × 12 = **84**
B   12 × 12 = **144**
D   5 × 12 = **60**
E   3 × 12 = **36**
I   11 × 12 = **132**

K   6 × 12 = **72**
M   2 × 12 = **24**
S   8 × 12 = **96**
T   9 × 12 = **108**
W   10 × 12 = **120**

Math Riddle: What did the spider do on the computer?

I T   M A D E   A   W E B S I T E
132 108   24 84 60 36   84   120 36 144 96 132 108 36

3. Find the missing factor.

7 × **12** = 84   2 × **12** = 24   3 × **12** = 36   **8** × 12 = 96
12 × 4 = 48   12 × **12** = 108   **5** × 12 = 60   12 × **11** = 132
10 × **12** = 120   **4** × 12 = 48   **6** × 12 = 72   **2** × 12 = 24
1 × 12 = 12   12 × **5** = 60   **0** × 12 = 0   **12** × 12 = 144

Multiply by 10, 11, and 12 — 43

1. Find the product. Colour odd products red. Colour even products blue.

9 ×10 = **108**	11 ×10 = **110**	9 ×11 = **99**	4 ×10 = **40**	4 ×12 = **48**
3 ×10 = **30**	5 ×11 = **55**	11 ×12 = **132**	7 ×10 = **70**	6 ×11 = **66**
5 ×10 = **50**	2 ×12 = **24**	7 ×11 = **77**	10 ×11 = **110**	3 ×12 = **36**
12 ×10 = **120**	5 ×12 = **60**	2 ×10 = **20**	6 ×12 = **72**	8 ×10 = **80**
3 ×11 = **33**	9 ×10 = **90**	12 ×11 = **132**	6 ×10 = **60**	8 ×11 = **88**
12 ×12 = **144**	4 ×11 = **44**	7 ×12 = **84**	11 ×11 = **121**	8 ×12 = **96**

Math Riddle: Multiplication Facts for 10, 11, and 12 — 44

How do you greet a two-headed alien?

N I C E | T O | M E E T | Y O U
72 84 55 96 | 20 90 | 121 96 96 20 | 48 90 77

N I C E | T O | M E E T | Y O U
72 84 55 96 | 20 90 | 121 96 96 20 | 48 90 77

A 12 ×10 = **120**	C 5 ×11 = **55**	D 11 ×10 = **110**	E 8 ×12 = **96**	G 6 ×11 = **66**
I 7 ×12 = **84**	L 10 ×10 = **100**	M 11 ×11 = **121**	N 6 ×12 = **72**	O 9 ×10 = **90**
P 3 ×11 = **33**	R 9 ×12 = **108**	T 2 ×10 = **20**	U 7 ×11 = **77**	Y 4 ×12 = **48**

Watch out! Not all of the letters are used in the answer.

Math Blaster—Multiplication Challenge 1 — 45

Multiply. How quickly can you solve these questions? Time yourself.

1. 2 × 7 = **14**
2. 3 × 6 = **18**
3. 11 × 4 = **44**
4. 2 × 8 = **16**
5. 0 × 9 = **0**
6. 8 × 6 = **48**
7. 9 × 10 = **90**
8. 7 × 6 = **42**
9. 8 × 8 = **64**
10. 6 × 9 = **54**
11. 4 × 4 = **16**
12. 5 × 1 = **5**
13. 4 × 7 = **28**
14. 9 × 2 = **18**
15. 7 × 3 = **21**
16. 0 × 11 = **0**
17. 1 × 2 = **2**
18. 6 × 8 = **48**
19. 5 × 7 = **35**
20. 10 × 10 = **100**

21. 9 × 5 = **45**
22. 7 × 2 = **14**
23. 9 × 12 = **108**
24. 1 × 9 = **9**
25. 7 × 5 = **35**
26. 0 × 6 = **0**
27. 8 × 2 = **16**
28. 4 × 1 = **4**
29. 6 × 6 = **36**
30. 5 × 8 = **40**
31. 8 × 3 = **24**
32. 3 × 3 = **9**
33. 5 × 6 = **30**
34. 1 × 5 = **5**
35. 7 × 7 = **49**
36. 9 × 9 = **81**
37. 2 × 5 = **10**
38. 0 × 4 = **0**
39. 9 × 3 = **27**
40. 12 × 12 = **144**

41. 12 × 7 = **84**
42. 7 × 2 = **14**
43. 9 × 11 = **99**
44. 11 × 10 = **110**
45. 2 × 0 = **0**
46. 4 × 5 = **20**
47. 6 × 7 = **42**
48. 8 × 11 = **88**
49. 3 × 8 = **24**
50. 10 × 10 = **100**

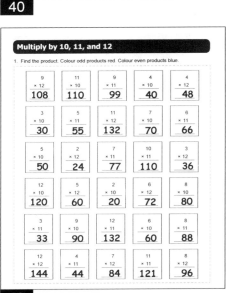

Time
_____

Math Blaster Score

46

Math Blaster—Multiplication Challenge 2

Multiply. How quickly can you solve these questions? Time yourself.

1. 6 × 3 = 18
2. 8 × 2 = 16
3. 10 × 5 = 50
4. 0 × 1 = 0
5. 7 × 4 = 28
6. 6 × 7 = 42
7. 11 × 4 = 44
8. 3 × 5 = 15
9. 2 × 2 = 4
10. 6 × 11 = 66
11. 9 × 9 = 81
12. 4 × 5 = 20
13. 5 × 5 = 25
14. 3 × 7 = 21
15. 9 × 8 = 72
16. 2 × 7 = 14
17. 2 × 6 = 12
18. 11 × 3 = 33
19. 9 × 3 = 27
20. 10 × 9 = 90
21. 9 × 1 = 9
22. 8 × 7 = 56
23. 2 × 1 = 2
24. 9 × 7 = 63
25. 4 × 6 = 24
26. 6 × 2 = 12
27. 7 × 8 = 56
28. 6 × 5 = 30
29. 12 × 1 = 12
30. 7 × 9 = 63
31. 4 × 3 = 12
32. 3 × 8 = 24
33. 1 × 6 = 6
34. 5 × 3 = 15
35. 6 × 9 = 54
36. 0 × 7 = 0
37. 12 × 10 = 120
38. 7 × 2 = 14
39. 8 × 5 = 40
40. 9 × 6 = 54
41. 12 × 6 = 72
42. 7 × 11 = 77
43. 9 × 9 = 81
44. 11 × 6 = 66
45. 2 × 11 = 22
46. 4 × 0 = 0
47. 6 × 1 = 6
48. 8 × 12 = 96
49. 2 × 10 = 20
50. 10 × 7 = 70

Time

Math Blaster Score

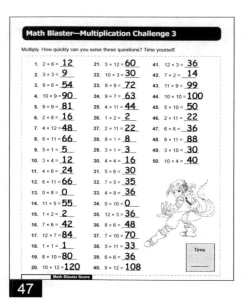

47

Math Blaster—Multiplication Challenge 3

Multiply. How quickly can you solve these questions? Time yourself.

1. 2 × 6 = 12
2. 3 × 3 = 9
3. 9 × 6 = 54
4. 10 × 9 = 90
5. 9 × 9 = 81
6. 2 × 8 = 16
7. 4 × 12 = 48
8. 6 × 11 = 66
9. 5 × 1 = 5
10. 3 × 4 = 12
11. 4 × 6 = 24
12. 6 × 11 = 66
13. 0 × 8 = 0
14. 11 × 5 = 55
15. 1 × 2 = 2
16. 7 × 6 = 42
17. 12 × 7 = 84
18. 1 × 1 = 1
19. 8 × 10 = 80
20. 10 × 12 = 120
21. 5 × 12 = 60
22. 10 × 3 = 30
23. 9 × 8 = 72
24. 9 × 7 = 63
25. 4 × 11 = 44
26. 1 × 2 = 2
27. 2 × 11 = 22
28. 8 × 1 = 8
29. 3 × 1 = 3
30. 4 × 4 = 16
31. 5 × 6 = 30
32. 7 × 5 = 35
33. 4 × 9 = 36
34. 0 × 10 = 0
35. 12 × 3 = 36
36. 8 × 6 = 48
37. 7 × 10 = 70
38. 3 × 11 = 33
39. 6 × 6 = 36
40. 9 × 12 = 108
41. 12 × 3 = 36
42. 7 × 2 = 14
43. 11 × 9 = 99
44. 10 × 10 = 100
45. 5 × 10 = 50
46. 2 × 11 = 22
47. 6 × 6 = 36
48. 8 × 11 = 88
49. 3 × 10 = 30
50. 10 × 4 = 40

Time

Math Blaster Score

48

Math Blaster—Multiplication Challenge 4

Multiply. How quickly can you solve these questions? Time yourself.

1. 12 × 12 = 144
2. 9 × 3 = 27
3. 4 × 7 = 28
4. 7 × 2 = 14
5. 3 × 10 = 30
6. 2 × 4 = 8
7. 5 × 8 = 40
8. 8 × 11 = 88
9. 10 × 9 = 90
10. 3 × 9 = 27
11. 5 × 7 = 35
12. 5 × 2 = 10
13. 11 × 10 = 110
14. 0 × 9 = 0
15. 6 × 5 = 30
16. 5 × 5 = 25
17. 11 × 12 = 132
18. 2 × 7 = 14
19. 7 × 4 = 28
20. 1 × 11 = 11
21. 9 × 5 = 45
22. 4 × 9 = 36
23. 7 × 3 = 21
24. 8 × 8 = 64
25. 4 × 12 = 48
26. 1 × 7 = 7
27. 2 × 10 = 20
28. 8 × 12 = 96
29. 10 × 10 = 100
30. 0 × 2 = 0
31. 2 × 2 = 4
32. 9 × 8 = 72
33. 4 × 6 = 24
34. 8 × 7 = 56
35. 11 × 11 = 121
36. 3 × 8 = 24
37. 5 × 1 = 5
38. 3 × 6 = 18
39. 5 × 12 = 60
40. 7 × 10 = 70
41. 12 × 7 = 84
42. 7 × 2 = 14
43. 9 × 11 = 99
44. 10 × 11 = 110
45. 2 × 0 = 0
46. 3 × 5 = 15
47. 6 × 7 = 42
48. 11 × 7 = 77
49. 3 × 8 = 24
50. 9 × 10 = 90

Time

Math Blaster Score

49

Math Blaster—Multiplication Challenge 5

Multiply. How quickly can you solve these questions? Time yourself.

1. 11 × 12 = 132
2. 8 × 3 = 24
3. 3 × 7 = 21
4. 6 × 2 = 12
5. 2 × 10 = 20
6. 1 × 4 = 4
7. 4 × 8 = 32
8. 7 × 11 = 77
9. 9 × 9 = 81
10. 2 × 9 = 18
11. 4 × 7 = 28
12. 4 × 2 = 8
13. 10 × 10 = 100
14. 1 × 9 = 9
15. 5 × 5 = 25
16. 4 × 5 = 20
17. 10 × 12 = 120
18. 0 × 7 = 0
19. 6 × 4 = 24
20. 0 × 11 = 0
21. 8 × 5 = 40
22. 3 × 9 = 27
23. 6 × 3 = 18
24. 7 × 8 = 56
25. 3 × 12 = 36
26. 1 × 7 = 7
27. 1 × 10 = 10
28. 7 × 12 = 84
29. 9 × 10 = 90
30. 12 × 2 = 24
31. 11 × 2 = 22
32. 8 × 8 = 64
33. 3 × 6 = 18
34. 7 × 7 = 49
35. 10 × 11 = 110
36. 2 × 8 = 16
37. 5 × 1 = 5
38. 2 × 6 = 12
39. 4 × 12 = 48
40. 6 × 10 = 60
41. 12 × 12 = 144
42. 2 × 7 = 14
43. 10 × 8 = 80
44. 5 × 10 = 50
45. 4 × 5 = 20
46. 6 × 12 = 72
47. 9 × 12 = 108
48. 8 × 8 = 64
49. 3 × 3 = 9
50. 12 × 11 = 132

Time

Math Blaster Score

50

Math Blaster 1—Multiplying by 1 to 6

4 × 6 = 24	4 × 4 = 16	6 × 5 = 30	7 × 6 = 42	4 × 1 = 4	12 × 3 = 36	10 × 2 = 20
3 × 1 = 3	11 × 2 = 22	7 × 2 = 14	4 × 5 = 20	8 × 3 = 24	7 × 4 = 28	9 × 2 = 18
6 × 6 = 36	6 × 3 = 18	12 × 2 = 24	1 × 4 = 4	5 × 5 = 25	8 × 5 = 40	Math Blaster Score /20

Math Blaster 2—Multiplying by 1 to 6

4 × 1 = 4	5 × 2 = 10	3 × 5 = 15	4 × 6 = 24	9 × 2 = 18	7 × 1 = 7	9 × 4 = 36
4 × 3 = 12	2 × 6 = 12	5 × 5 = 25	8 × 6 = 48	5 × 3 = 15	6 × 4 = 24	8 × 3 = 24
10 × 4 = 40	7 × 3 = 21	12 × 5 = 60	1 × 1 = 1	6 × 2 = 12	11 × 2 = 22	Math Blaster Score /20

51

Math Blaster 3—Multiplying by 1 to 6

11 × 6 = 66	5 × 3 = 15	9 × 5 = 45	12 × 4 = 48	1 × 2 = 2	8 × 3 = 24	10 × 2 = 20
6 × 3 = 18	8 × 5 = 40	2 × 1 = 2	4 × 4 = 16	3 × 3 = 9	4 × 5 = 20	7 × 6 = 42
6 × 2 = 12	11 × 3 = 33	5 × 5 = 25	9 × 6 = 54	8 × 1 = 8	6 × 4 = 24	Math Blaster Score /20

Math Blaster 4—Multiplying by 1 to 6

3 × 1 = 3	5 × 6 = 30	3 × 2 = 6	8 × 4 = 32	3 × 3 = 9	12 × 5 = 60	10 × 5 = 50
9 × 1 = 9	2 × 1 = 2	11 × 4 = 44	10 × 6 = 60	8 × 5 = 40	6 × 3 = 18	7 × 3 = 21
5 × 4 = 20	7 × 2 = 14	6 × 5 = 30	10 × 3 = 30	9 × 2 = 18	8 × 6 = 48	Math Blaster Score /20

52

Math Blaster 5—Multiplying by 1 to 6

6 × 4 = 24	3 × 2 = 6	11 × 1 = 11	7 × 6 = 42	12 × 3 = 36	9 × 2 = 18	9 × 5 = 45
5 × 6 = 30	3 × 4 = 12	6 × 5 = 30	4 × 2 = 8	10 × 3 = 30	4 × 5 = 20	7 × 2 = 14
4 × 4 = 16	1 × 2 = 2	2 × 5 = 10	2 × 3 = 6	8 × 1 = 8	12 × 6 = 72	Math Blaster Score /20

Math Blaster 6—Multiplying by 1 to 6

3 × 4 = 12	5 × 3 = 15	11 × 5 = 55	5 × 1 = 5	8 × 6 = 48	1 × 2 = 2	8 × 4 = 32
6 × 6 = 36	8 × 1 = 8	6 × 5 = 30	3 × 3 = 9	7 × 2 = 14	5 × 4 = 20	10 × 4 = 40
2 × 5 = 10	3 × 2 = 6	12 × 6 = 72	8 × 3 = 24	12 × 1 = 12	9 × 4 = 36	Math Blaster Score /20

53

Math Blaster 7—Multiplying by 1 to 6

9 × 2 = 18	11 × 3 = 33	7 × 6 = 42	8 × 4 = 32	2 × 1 = 2	4 × 3 = 12	2 × 5 = 10
6 × 2 = 12	12 × 4 = 48	7 × 3 = 21	5 × 2 = 10	12 × 6 = 72	1 × 1 = 1	6 × 5 = 30
10 × 1 = 10	5 × 6 = 30	10 × 5 = 50	1 × 3 = 3	6 × 4 = 24	9 × 3 = 27	Math Blaster Score /20

Math Blaster 8—Multiplying by 1 to 6

3 × 4 = 12	5 × 3 = 15	3 × 2 = 6	11 × 6 = 66	6 × 5 = 30	10 × 4 = 40	8 × 4 = 32
5 × 4 = 20	4 × 6 = 24	12 × 5 = 60	4 × 2 = 8	3 × 3 = 9	3 × 1 = 3	7 × 3 = 21
5 × 2 = 10	10 × 2 = 20	1 × 6 = 6	8 × 5 = 40	9 × 3 = 27	4 × 3 = 12	Math Blaster Score /20

54

Math Blaster 9—Multiplying by 1 to 6

6 × 4 = 24	11 × 2 = 22	5 × 1 = 5	7 × 5 = 35	6 × 6 = 36	12 × 2 = 24	8 × 6 = 48
3 × 2 = 6	11 × 3 = 33	3 × 6 = 18	8 × 2 = 16	4 × 3 = 12	9 × 4 = 36	7 × 4 = 28
10 × 5 = 50	2 × 4 = 8	9 × 2 = 18	8 × 3 = 24	12 × 6 = 72	9 × 5 = 45	Math Blaster Score /20

Math Blaster 10—Multiplying by 1 to 6

5 × 5 = 25	6 × 6 = 36	12 × 3 = 36	2 × 2 = 4	1 × 4 = 4	7 × 2 = 14	10 × 2 = 20
6 × 2 = 12	2 × 1 = 2	8 × 3 = 24	4 × 5 = 20	2 × 6 = 12	10 × 1 = 10	3 × 4 = 12
9 × 6 = 54	11 × 5 = 55	4 × 3 = 12	7 × 4 = 28	5 × 2 = 10	9 × 4 = 36	Math Blaster Score /20

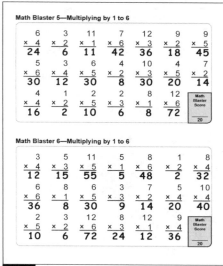

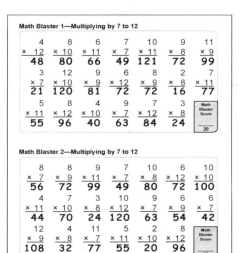
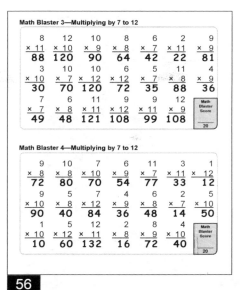
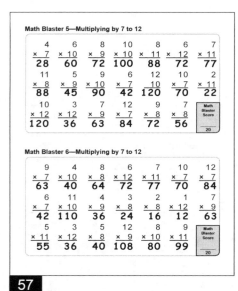

Math Blaster 1—Multiplying by 7 to 12 (55)

4 ×12 = 48	8 ×10 = 80	6 ×11 = 66	7 ×7 = 49	10 ×11 = 121	9 ×8 = 72	11 ×9 = 99
3 ×7 = 21	12 ×10 = 120	9 ×9 = 81	6 ×12 = 72	8 ×9 = 72	2 ×8 = 16	7 ×11 = 77
5 ×11 = 55	8 ×12 = 96	4 ×10 = 40	9 ×7 = 63	7 ×12 = 84	3 ×8 = 24	Math Blaster Score 20

Math Blaster 2—Multiplying by 7 to 12

8 ×7 = 56	8 ×9 = 72	9 ×11 = 99	7 ×7 = 49	10 ×8 = 80	6 ×12 = 72	10 ×10 = 100
4 ×11 = 44	7 ×10 = 70	3 ×8 = 24	10 ×12 = 120	9 ×7 = 63	6 ×9 = 54	6 ×7 = 42
12 ×9 = 108	4 ×8 = 32	11 ×7 = 77	5 ×11 = 55	2 ×10 = 20	8 ×12 = 96	Math Blaster Score 20

Math Blaster 3—Multiplying by 7 to 12 (56)

8 ×11 = 88	12 ×10 = 120	10 ×9 = 90	8 ×8 = 64	6 ×7 = 42	2 ×11 = 22	9 ×9 = 81
3 ×10 = 30	10 ×7 = 70	10 ×12 = 120	6 ×12 = 72	5 ×7 = 35	11 ×8 = 88	4 ×9 = 36
7 ×7 = 49	6 ×8 = 48	11 ×11 = 121	9 ×12 = 108	9 ×11 = 99	12 ×9 = 108	Math Blaster Score 20

Math Blaster 4—Multiplying by 7 to 12

9 ×8 = 72	10 ×8 = 80	7 ×10 = 70	6 ×9 = 54	11 ×7 = 77	3 ×11 = 33	1 ×12 = 12
9 ×10 = 90	5 ×8 = 40	7 ×12 = 84	4 ×9 = 36	6 ×8 = 48	2 ×7 = 14	5 ×10 = 50
1 ×10 = 10	5 ×12 = 60	12 ×11 = 132	2 ×8 = 16	8 ×9 = 72	4 ×10 = 40	Math Blaster Score 20

Math Blaster 5—Multiplying by 7 to 12 (57)

4 ×7 = 28	6 ×10 = 60	8 ×9 = 72	10 ×10 = 100	8 ×11 = 88	6 ×12 = 72	7 ×11 = 77
11 ×8 = 88	5 ×9 = 45	9 ×10 = 90	6 ×7 = 42	12 ×10 = 120	10 ×7 = 70	2 ×11 = 22
10 ×12 = 120	3 ×12 = 36	7 ×9 = 63	12 ×7 = 84	9 ×8 = 72	7 ×8 = 56	Math Blaster Score 20

Math Blaster 6—Multiplying by 7 to 12

9 ×7 = 63	4 ×10 = 40	8 ×8 = 64	6 ×12 = 72	7 ×11 = 77	10 ×7 = 70	12 ×7 = 84
6 ×7 = 42	11 ×10 = 110	4 ×9 = 36	3 ×8 = 24	2 ×8 = 16	1 ×12 = 12	7 ×9 = 63
5 ×11 = 55	3 ×12 = 36	5 ×8 = 40	12 ×9 = 108	8 ×10 = 80	9 ×11 = 99	Math Blaster Score 20

Math Blaster 7—Multiplying by 7 to 12 (58)

9 ×10 = 90	7 ×8 = 56	6 ×7 = 42	10 ×10 = 100	3 ×8 = 24	6 ×9 = 54	8 ×9 = 72
7 ×7 = 49	12 ×9 = 108	8 ×12 = 96	3 ×11 = 33	1 ×8 = 8	9 ×7 = 63	12 ×10 = 120
6 ×8 = 48	11 ×9 = 99	2 ×12 = 24	7 ×9 = 63	4 ×11 = 44	5 ×10 = 50	Math Blaster Score 20

Math Blaster 8—Multiplying by 7 to 12

6 ×11 = 66	8 ×8 = 64	7 ×9 = 63	10 ×7 = 70	2 ×10 = 20	11 ×7 = 77	6 ×12 = 72
4 ×10 = 40	8 ×10 = 80	10 ×9 = 90	6 ×8 = 48	1 ×7 = 7	5 ×12 = 60	4 ×9 = 36
12 ×7 = 84	5 ×12 = 60	7 ×7 = 49	4 ×11 = 44	3 ×8 = 24	9 ×9 = 81	Math Blaster Score 20

Math Blaster 9—Multiplying by 7 to 12 (59)

2 ×7 = 14	7 ×12 = 84	9 ×9 = 81	8 ×8 = 64	6 ×11 = 66	10 ×11 = 110	10 ×9 = 90
8 ×11 = 88	3 ×11 = 33	6 ×8 = 48	11 ×12 = 132	5 ×7 = 35	2 ×8 = 16	4 ×9 = 36
4 ×10 = 40	12 ×7 = 84	7 ×8 = 56	4 ×12 = 48	1 ×10 = 10	9 ×10 = 90	Math Blaster Score 20

Math Blaster 10—Multiplying by 7 to 12

9 ×9 = 81	4 ×12 = 48	11 ×8 = 88	9 ×11 = 99	8 ×10 = 80	3 ×7 = 21	1 ×10 = 10
10 ×7 = 70	7 ×8 = 56	2 ×7 = 14	8 ×12 = 96	9 ×10 = 90	10 ×11 = 110	7 ×7 = 49
5 ×8 = 40	2 ×10 = 20	6 ×12 = 72	3 ×9 = 27	10 ×9 = 90	11 ×12 = 132	Math Blaster Score 20

Math Blaster 1—Multiplying by 1 to 12 (60)

7 ×5 = 35	4 ×6 = 24	9 ×9 = 81	5 ×3 = 15	8 ×2 = 16	2 ×4 = 8	10 ×7 = 70
4 ×9 = 36	9 ×10 = 90	12 ×6 = 72	4 ×4 = 16	7 ×8 = 56	10 ×1 = 10	5 ×8 = 40
6 ×5 = 30	10 ×2 = 20	3 ×7 = 21	2 ×5 = 10	12 ×12 = 144	11 ×11 = 121	Math Blaster Score 20

Math Blaster 2—Multiplying by 1 to 12

8 ×5 = 40	7 ×6 = 42	11 ×10 = 110	3 ×4 = 12	9 ×8 = 72	6 ×6 = 36	4 ×9 = 36
10 ×10 = 100	12 ×1 = 12	6 ×4 = 24	6 ×2 = 12	3 ×11 = 33	8 ×7 = 56	3 ×8 = 24
5 ×2 = 10	6 ×7 = 42	4 ×12 = 48	1 ×5 = 5	2 ×2 = 4	7 ×3 = 21	Math Blaster Score 20

Math Blaster 3—Multiplying by 1 to 12 (61)

9 ×3 = 27	4 ×1 = 4	10 ×6 = 60	11 ×11 = 121	8 ×7 = 56	12 ×9 = 108	8 ×10 = 80
9 ×4 = 36	11 ×5 = 55	6 ×8 = 48	8 ×4 = 32	4 ×2 = 8	11 ×8 = 88	5 ×7 = 35
9 ×2 = 18	10 ×12 = 120	7 ×3 = 21	6 ×9 = 54	5 ×5 = 25	2 ×6 = 12	Math Blaster Score 20

Math Blaster 4—Multiplying by 1 to 12

7 ×9 = 63	5 ×12 = 60	4 ×4 = 16	6 ×8 = 48	3 ×7 = 21	12 ×3 = 36	7 ×10 = 70
2 ×5 = 10	11 ×1 = 11	2 ×7 = 14	6 ×5 = 30	10 ×8 = 80	9 ×6 = 54	8 ×5 = 40
3 ×2 = 6	3 ×6 = 18	7 ×11 = 77	5 ×4 = 20	7 ×2 = 14	1 ×8 = 8	Math Blaster Score 20

Math Blaster 5—Multiplying by 1 to 12 (62)

10 ×9 = 90	1 ×2 = 2	9 ×8 = 72	6 ×4 = 24	5 ×7 = 35	3 ×3 = 9	7 ×9 = 63
3 ×4 = 12	11 ×9 = 99	3 ×5 = 15	8 ×6 = 48	5 ×9 = 45	6 ×10 = 60	8 ×12 = 96
7 ×3 = 21	10 ×12 = 120	6 ×11 = 66	7 ×6 = 42	12 ×2 = 24	9 ×1 = 9	Math Blaster Score 20

Math Blaster 6—Multiplying by 1 to 12

7 ×5 = 35	12 ×12 = 144	5 ×10 = 50	3 ×9 = 27	9 ×7 = 63	6 ×8 = 48	2 ×8 = 16
10 ×4 = 40	4 ×4 = 16	9 ×9 = 81	3 ×6 = 18	10 ×2 = 20	5 ×9 = 45	7 ×11 = 77
12 ×3 = 36	1 ×12 = 12	10 ×3 = 30	11 ×8 = 88	5 ×1 = 5	7 ×6 = 42	Math Blaster Score 20

Math Blaster 7—Multiplying by 1 to 12 (63)

4 ×10 = 40	12 ×2 = 24	9 ×7 = 63	9 ×5 = 45	10 ×12 = 120	9 ×6 = 54	11 ×9 = 99
4 ×1 = 4	5 ×12 = 60	2 ×3 = 6	9 ×8 = 72	7 ×6 = 42	4 ×10 = 40	3 ×11 = 33
6 ×3 = 18	1 ×9 = 9	11 ×8 = 88	7 ×3 = 21	5 ×6 = 30	2 ×7 = 14	Math Blaster Score 20

Math Blaster 8—Multiplying by 1 to 12

6 ×7 = 42	12 ×7 = 84	4 ×9 = 36	5 ×11 = 55	3 ×8 = 24	5 ×12 = 60	9 ×8 = 72
10 ×5 = 50	5 ×1 = 5	7 ×7 = 49	4 ×4 = 12	11 ×6 = 66	2 ×3 = 6	12 ×11 = 132
6 ×9 = 54	8 ×10 = 20	12 ×2 = 16	9 ×8 = 96	4 ×10 = 81	40	Math Blaster Score 20

Math Blaster 9—Multiplying by 1 to 12

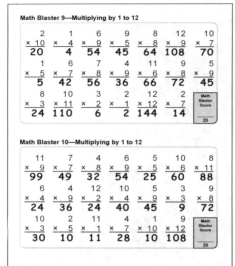

2 × 10 = **20**	1 × 4 = **4**	6 × 9 = **54**	9 × 5 = **45**	8 × 8 = **64**	12 × 9 = **108**	10 × 7 = **70**
1 × 5 = **5**	6 × 7 = **42**	7 × 8 = **56**	4 × 9 = **36**	11 × 6 = **66**	9 × 8 = **72**	5 × 9 = **45**
8 × 3 = **24**	10 × 11 = **110**	3 × 2 = **6**	2 × 1 = **2**	12 × 12 = **144**	2 × 7 = **14**	

Math Blaster Score **20**

Math Blaster 10—Multiplying by 1 to 12

11 × 9 = **99**	7 × 7 = **49**	4 × 8 = **32**	6 × 9 = **54**	5 × 5 = **25**	10 × 6 = **60**	8 × 11 = **88**
6 × 4 = **24**	4 × 9 = **36**	12 × 2 = **24**	10 × 4 = **40**	5 × 9 = **45**	3 × 3 = **9**	8 × 9 = **72**
10 × 3 = **30**	2 × 5 = **10**	11 × 1 = **11**	4 × 7 = **28**	1 × 10 = **10**	9 × 12 = **108**	

Math Blaster Score **20**

64

Multiply by Tens

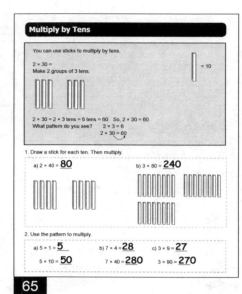

You can use sticks to multiply by tens.

2 × 30 =
Make 2 groups of 3 tens.

= 10

2 × 30 = 2 × 3 tens = 6 tens = 60. So, 2 × 30 = 60.
What pattern do you see?   2 × 3 = 6
                             2 × 30 = 60

1. Draw a stick for each ten. Then multiply.

a) 2 × 40 = **80**

b) 3 × 80 = **240**

2. Use the pattern to multiply.

a) 5 × 1 = **5**   b) 7 × 4 = **28**   c) 3 × 9 = **27**
   5 × 10 = **50**   7 × 40 = **280**   3 × 90 = **270**

65

Multiply by Hundreds

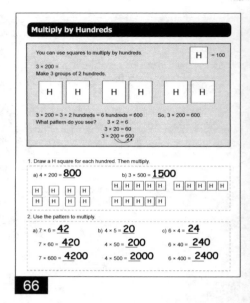

You can use squares to multiply by hundreds.

H = 100

3 × 200 =
Make 3 groups of 2 hundreds.

3 × 200 = 3 × 2 hundreds = 6 hundreds = 600.   So, 3 × 200 = 600.
What pattern do you see?   3 × 2 = 6
                             3 × 20 = 60
                             3 × 200 = 600

1. Draw a H square for each hundred. Then multiply.

a) 4 × 200 = **800**

b) 3 × 500 = **1500**

2. Use the pattern to multiply.

a) 7 × 6 = **42**   b) 4 × 5 = **20**   c) 6 × 4 = **24**
   7 × 60 = **420**   4 × 50 = **200**   6 × 40 = **240**
   7 × 600 = **4200**   4 × 500 = **2000**   6 × 400 = **2400**

66

Multiply by Thousands

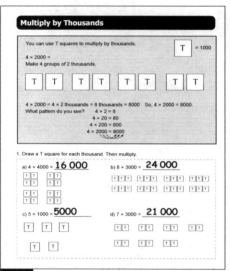

You can use T squares to multiply by thousands.

T = 1000

4 × 2000 =
Make 4 groups of 2 thousands.

4 × 2000 = 4 × 2 thousands = 8 thousands = 8000.   So, 4 × 2000 = 8000.
What pattern do you see?   4 × 2 = 8
                             4 × 20 = 80
                             4 × 200 = 800
                             4 × 2000 = 8000

1. Draw a T square for each thousand. Then multiply.

a) 4 × 4000 = **16 000**

b) 8 × 3000 = **24 000**

c) 5 × 1000 = **5000**

d) 7 × 3000 = **21 000**

67

Multiply Multiples of 10, 100, and 1000

Multiply   7 × 5000 = _____
7 × 5 ones = 35 ones = **35**
7 × 5 tens = 35 tens = **350**
7 × 5 hundreds = 35 hundreds = **3500**
7 × 5 thousands = 35 thousands = **35 000**
So 7 × 5000 = **35 000**

1. Use multiplication facts and patterns to help you multiply.

a) 5 × 4 = **20**   b) 8 × 7 = **56**   c) 9 × 2 = **18**
   5 × 40 = **200**   8 × 70 = **560**   9 × 20 = **180**
   5 × 400 = **2000**   8 × 700 = **5600**   9 × 200 = **1800**
   5 × 4000 = **20 000**   8 × 7000 = **56 000**   9 × 2000 = **18 000**

d) 6 × 6 = **36**   e) 4 × 7 = **28**   f) 3 × 4 = **12**
   6 × 60 = **360**   4 × 70 = **280**   3 × 40 = **120**
   6 × 600 = **3600**   4 × 700 = **2800**   3 × 400 = **1200**
   6 × 6000 = **36 000**   4 × 7000 = **28 000**   3 × 4000 = **12 000**

g) 6 × 8 = **48**   h) 2 × 5 = **10**   I) 7 × 5 = **35**
   6 × 80 = **480**   2 × 50 = **100**   7 × 50 = **350**
   6 × 800 = **4800**   2 × 500 = **1000**   7 × 500 = **3500**
   6 × 8000 = **48 000**   2 × 5000 = **10 000**   7 × 5000 = **35 000**

68

Multiply Multiples of 10, 100, and 1000 (continued)

2. Use the pattern to multiply.

a) 2 × 7 = **14**   b) 8 × 3 = **24**   c) 9 × 9 = **81**
   2 × 70 = **140**   8 × 30 = **240**   9 × 90 = **810**
   2 × 700 = **1400**   8 × 300 = **2400**   9 × 900 = **8100**
   2 × 7000 = **14 000**   8 × 3000 = **24 000**   9 × 9000 = **81 000**

d) 5 × 3 = **15**   e) 5 × 8 = **40**   f) 6 × 5 = **30**
   5 × 30 = **150**   5 × 80 = **400**   6 × 50 = **300**
   5 × 300 = **1500**   5 × 800 = **4000**   6 × 500 = **3000**
   5 × 3000 = **15 000**   5 × 8000 = **40 000**   6 × 5000 = **30 000**

3. Multiply.

a) 5 × 50 = **250**   b) 7 × 300 = **2100**   c) 8 × 1000 = **8000**
d) 7 × 200 = **1400**   e) 5 × 40 = **200**   f) 7 × 700 = **4900**
g) 5 × 500 = **2500**   h) 6 × 80 = **480**   i) 8 × 500 = **4000**
j) 3 × 80 = **240**   k) 2 × 1000 = **2000**   l) 9 × 400 = **3600**
m) 6 × 900 = **5400**   n) 4 × 30 = **120**   o) 4 × 1000 = **4000**
p) 3 × 6000 = **18 000** q) 9 × 900 = **8100**   r) 1 × 50 = **50**

69

Multiply Two-digit Numbers by One-digit Numbers

Step 1: Multiply the ones.

6 ones × 9 ones = 54 ones
Regroup 54 as 5 tens and 4 ones.

5
1 6
× 9
4

Step 2: Multiply the tens.

1 ten × 9 ones = 9 tens
Then add the regrouped 5 tens.
9 tens + 5 tens = 14 tens

5
1 6
× 9
1 4 4

1 hundred + 4 tens + 4 ones

1. Multiply. Regroup where necessary. Hint: Make sure to line up the numbers.

44 × 3 = **132**	16 × 4 = **64**	38 × 5 = **190**	69 × 2 = **138**
17 × 8 = **136**	54 × 6 = **324**	27 × 9 = **243**	76 × 4 = **304**
49 × 2 = **98**	56 × 8 = **448**	99 × 5 = **495**	32 × 2 = **64**

70

Multiply Two-digit Numbers by One-digit Numbers (continued)

2. Multiply. Regroup where necessary. Hint: Make sure to line up the numbers.

95 × 2 = **190**	50 × 4 = **200**	67 × 9 = **603**	45 × 5 = **225**
76 × 4 = **304**	84 × 5 = **420**	97 × 8 = **776**	64 × 3 = **192**
68 × 2 = **136**	19 × 4 = **76**	77 × 3 = **231**	55 × 9 = **495**
83 × 8 = **664**	92 × 7 = **644**	79 × 6 = **474**	46 × 3 = **138**
25 × 9 = **225**	52 × 2 = **104**	31 × 6 = **186**	87 × 4 = **348**

Math Blaster Score

71

Multiply Two-digit Numbers by One-digit Numbers (continued)

3. Multiply. Regroup where necessary. Hint: Make sure to line up the numbers.

38 × 2 = **76**	56 × 5 = **280**	78 × 7 = **546**	63 × 9 = **567**
42 × 6 = **252**	80 × 4 = **320**	97 × 3 = **291**	26 × 5 = **130**
74 × 8 = **592**	76 × 4 = **304**	55 × 7 = **385**	66 × 9 = **594**
32 × 4 = **128**	88 × 8 = **704**	91 × 3 = **273**	65 × 2 = **130**
27 × 5 = **135**	64 × 2 = **128**	43 × 9 = **387**	33 × 6 = **198**

Math Blaster Score

72

Multiply Two-digit Numbers by One-digit Numbers (continued)

4. Multiply. Regroup where necessary. Hint: Make sure to line up the numbers.

64 × 2 = **128**	17 × 4 = **68**	90 × 9 = **810**	35 × 5 = **175**
83 × 4 = **332**	76 × 5 = **380**	49 × 8 = **392**	51 × 3 = **153**
28 × 2 = **56**	54 × 4 = **216**	89 × 3 = **267**	60 × 9 = **540**
72 × 8 = **576**	19 × 7 = **133**	87 × 6 = **522**	76 × 3 = **228**
98 × 9 = **882**	44 × 2 = **88**	61 × 6 = **366**	50 × 4 = **200**

73

Multiply Two-digit Numbers by One-digit Numbers (continued)

5. Multiply. Regroup where necessary. Hint: Make sure to line up the numbers.

26 × 7 = **182**	19 × 5 = **95**	82 × 5 = **410**	44 × 9 = **396**
33 × 6 = **198**	75 × 4 = **300**	21 × 3 = **63**	57 × 5 = **285**
80 × 8 = **640**	39 × 4 = **156**	17 × 7 = **119**	25 × 9 = **225**
42 × 4 = **168**	98 × 8 = **784**	51 × 3 = **153**	35 × 2 = **70**
17 × 5 = **85**	28 × 2 = **56**	54 × 9 = **486**	60 × 6 = **360**

74

Multiply Multi-digit Numbers

Step 1: Multiply the ones. 6 ones × 5 ones = 30 ones. Regroup 30 as 3 tens and 0 ones.

Step 2: Multiply the tens. 1 ten × 5 ones = 5 tens. Then add the regrouped 3 tens. 5 tens + 3 tens = 8 tens.

Step 3: Multiply the hundreds. 3 hundreds × 5 ones = 15 hundreds. Regroup 1500 as 1 thousand and 5 hundreds. Since there are no other thousands, write the "1" in the answer.

316 × 5 = 1580

1. Multiply. Regroup where necessary. Check your work.

314 × 3 = **942**	708 × 2 = **1416**	497 × 5 = **2485**	135 × 4 = **540**
268 × 7 = **1876**	910 × 6 = **5460**	601 × 8 = **4808**	244 × 9 = **2196**

75

Multiply Multi-digit Numbers—Challenge 1

Multiply. Regroup where necessary. Check your work.

752 × 6 = **4512**	214 × 3 = **642**	671 × 4 = **2684**	890 × 5 = **4450**
925 × 2 = **1850**	607 × 6 = **3642**	453 × 3 = **1359**	570 × 7 = **3990**
165 × 9 = **1485**	875 × 5 = **4375**	346 × 8 = **2768**	604 × 6 = **3624**
7341 × 2 = **4682**	2764 × 3 = **8292**	1528 × 5 = **7640**	9032 × 4 = **38 128**
3420 × 8 = **27 360**	5451 × 7 = **38 157**	6109 × 6 = **36 654**	7815 × 9 = **70 335**

76

Multiply Multi-digit Numbers—Challenge 2

Multiply. Regroup where necessary. Check your work.

553 × 6 = **3318**	306 × 3 = **918**	890 × 4 = **3560**	418 × 5 = **2090**
761 × 2 = **1522**	547 × 6 = **3282**	178 × 8 = **1424**	634 × 7 = **4438**
275 × 9 = **2475**	982 × 5 = **4910**	174 × 8 = **1392**	323 × 6 = **1938**
5672 × 2 = **11 344**	2534 × 3 = **7602**	3675 × 5 = **18 375**	1906 × 4 = **7624**
8941 × 8 = **71 528**	4783 × 7 = **33 481**	9750 × 6 = **58 500**	4389 × 9 = **39 501**

77

Multiply Multi-digit Numbers—Challenge 3

Multiply. Regroup where necessary. Check your work.

591 × 8 = **4728**	824 × 3 = **2472**	340 × 4 = **1360**	469 × 4 = **1876**
161 × 2 = **322**	945 × 6 = **5670**	278 × 8 = **2224**	534 × 7 = **3738**
675 × 9 = **6075**	234 × 5 = **1170**	908 × 8 = **7264**	423 × 7 = **2961**
8032 × 2 = **16 064**	4860 × 3 = **14 580**	9541 × 5 = **47 705**	1908 × 4 = **7632**
2943 × 5 = **14 715**	5694 × 7 = **39 858**	3628 × 6 = **21 768**	6785 × 4 = **27 140**

78

Multiply Multi-digit Numbers—Challenge 4

Multiply. Regroup where necessary. Check your work.

893 × 8 = **7144**	104 × 4 = **416**	279 × 2 = **558**	385 × 5 = **1925**
943 × 9 = **8487**	217 × 8 = **1736**	985 × 7 = **6895**	539 × 3 = **1617**
408 × 9 = **3672**	743 × 5 = **3715**	360 × 5 = **1800**	173 × 6 = **1038**
6541 × 5 = **32 705**	8347 × 3 = **25 041**	1954 × 9 = **17 586**	2083 × 6 = **12 498**
7123 × 3 = **21 369**	5904 × 4 = **23 616**	4670 × 7 = **32 690**	9082 × 9 = **81 738**

79

Multiply Multi-digit Numbers—Challenge 5

Multiply. Regroup where necessary. Check your work.

208 × 4 = **832**	972 × 3 = **2916**	390 × 9 = **3510**	758 × 5 = **3790**
861 × 2 = **1722**	183 × 8 = **1464**	547 × 8 = **4376**	436 × 7 = **3052**
567 × 5 = **2835**	907 × 5 = **4535**	674 × 7 = **4718**	501 × 6 = **3006**
2509 × 2 = **5018**	1423 × 6 = **8538**	4786 × 5 = **23 930**	3028 × 2 = **6056**
6720 × 5 = **33 600**	8127 × 7 = **56 889**	4305 × 6 = **25 830**	5490 × 4 = **21 960**

80

Multiplication by 10, 100, and 1000—Challenge 1

Multiply.

#	Problem	#	Problem
1.	3 × 300 = **900**	21.	5 × 100 = **500**
2.	1 × 20 = **20**	22.	8 × 300 = **2400**
3.	2 × 3000 = **6000**	23.	4 × 50 = **200**
4.	7 × 50 = **350**	24.	5 × 1000 = **5000**
5.	4 × 800 = **3200**	25.	4 × 200 = **800**
6.	5 × 4000 = **20 000**	26.	1 × 30 = **30**
7.	6 × 20 = **120**	27.	3 × 600 = **1800**
8.	7 × ... = **800**	28.	7 × 600 = **4200**
9.	2 × 7000 = **14 000**	29.	10 × 40 = **400**
10.	3 × 70 = **210**	30.	1 × 2000 = **2000**
11.	9 × 600 = **5400**	31.	5 × 9000 = **45 000**
12.	7 × 7000 = **49 000**	32.	7 × 90 = **630**
13.	8 × 40 = **320**	33.	9 × 300 = **2700**
14.	7 × 700 = **4900**	34.	10 × 8000 = **80 000**
15.	5 × 6000 = **30 000**	35.	9 × 70 = **630**
16.	9 × 500 = **4500**	36.	8 × 700 = **5600**
17.	10 × 800 = **8000**	37.	3 × 7000 = **21 000**
18.	1 × 2000 = **2000**	38.	2 × 2000 = **4000**
19.	4 × 80 = **320**	39.	4 × 400 = **1600**
20.	10 × 50 = **500**	40.	9 × 40 = **360**

81

Multiplication by 10, 100, and 1000—Challenge 2

Multiply.

1. 1 × 90 = 90
2. 3 × 400 = 1200
3. 2 × 7000 = 14 000
4. 7 × 80 = 560
5. 4 × 700 = 2800
6. 5 × 3000 = 15 000
7. 6 × 60 = 360
8. 8 × 500 = 4000
9. 2 × 9000 = 18 000
10. 3 × 60 = 180
11. 9 × 900 = 8100
12. 7 × 7000 = 49 000
13. 8 × 200 = 1600
14. 7 × 50 = 350
15. 6 × 5000 = 30 000
16. 4 × 500 = 2000
17. 10 × 70 = 700
18. 1 × 4000 = 4000
19. 4 × 30 = 120
20. 10 × 800 = 8000
21. 5 × 8000 = 40 000
22. 8 × 600 = 4800
23. 4 × 20 = 80
24. 5 × 1000 = 5000
25. 4 × 900 = 3600
26. 12 × 10 = 120
27. 3 × 300 = 900
28. 7 × 6000 = 42 000
29. 10 × 80 = 800
30. 1 × 2000 = 2000
31. 5 × 500 = 2500
32. 7 × 40 = 280
33. 9 × 100 = 900
34. 10 × 7000 = 70 000
35. 9 × 20 = 180
36. 8 × 400 = 3200
37. 7 × 2000 = 14 000
38. 3 × 2000 = 6000
39. 4 × 600 = 2400
40. 9 × 60 = 540

82

Multiplication by 10, 100, and 1000—Challenge 3

Multiply.

1. 1 × 30 = 30
2. 4 × 300 = 1200
3. 2 × 8000 = 16 000
4. 9 × 50 = 450
5. 5 × 600 = 3000
6. 5 × 8000 = 40 000
7. 6 × 40 = 240
8. 8 × 50 = 400
9. 2 × 2000 = 4000
10. 3 × 7000 = 21 000
11. 4 × 600 = 2400
12. 6 × 8000 = 48 000
13. 10 × 100 = 1000
14. 4 × 300 = 1200
15. 5 × 7000 = 35 000
16. 8 × 500 = 4000
17. 1 × 90 = 90
18. 10 × 2000 = 20 000
19. 4 × 10 = 40
20. 12 × 800 = 9600
21. 9 × 9000 = 81 000
22. 12 × 600 = 7200
23. 5 × 50 = 250
24. 7 × 9000 = 63 000
25. 3 × 400 = 1200
26. 1 × 70 = 70
27. 6 × 600 = 3600
28. 7 × 400 = 2800
29. 11 × 40 = 440
30. 5 × 9000 = 45 000
31. 8 × 100 = 800
32. 10 × 90 = 900
33. 9 × 200 = 1800
34. 20 × 800 = 16 000
35. 7 × 70 = 490
36. 3 × 500 = 1500
37. 6 × 7000 = 42 000
38. 11 × 2000 = 22 000
39. 1 × 200 = 200
40. 9 × 90 = 810

83

Multiplication by 10, 100, and 1000—Challenge 4

Multiply.

1. 5 × 30 = 150
2. 7 × 300 = 2100
3. 9 × 8000 = 72 000
4. 2 × 50 = 100
5. 1 × 600 = 600
6. 4 × 8000 = 32 000
7. 12 × 40 = 480
8. 3 × 50 = 150
9. 3 × 2000 = 6000
10. 11 × 7000 = 77 000
11. 10 × 600 = 6000
12. 3 × 8000 = 24 000
13. 4 × 100 = 400
14. 12 × 300 = 3600
15. 4 × 7000 = 28 000
16. 9 × 500 = 4500
17. 8 × 90 = 720
18. 11 × 2000 = 22 000
19. 4 × 70 = 280
20. 11 × 700 = 7700
21. 4 × 9000 = 36 000
22. 7 × 600 = 4200
23. 4 × 50 = 200
24. 4 × 9000 = 36 000
25. 12 × 400 = 4800
26. 11 × 70 = 770
27. 2 × 600 = 1200
28. 6 × 400 = 2400
29. 9 × 40 = 360
30. 10 × 9000 = 90 000
31. 4 × 100 = 400
32. 6 × 90 = 540
33. 8 × 200 = 1600
34. 7 × 8000 = 56 000
35. 10 × 70 = 700
36. 7 × 500 = 3500
37. 2 × 7000 = 14 000
38. 1 × 2000 = 2000
39. 3 × 200 = 600
40. 4 × 90 = 360

84

Multiplication by 10, 100, and 1000—Challenge 5

Multiply.

1. 1 × 50 = 50
2. 4 × 400 = 1600
3. 2 × 6000 = 12 000
4. 9 × 40 = 360
5. 5 × 900 = 4500
6. 5 × 3000 = 15 000
7. 6 × 90 = 540
8. 10 × 30 = 300
9. 3 × 3000 = 9000
10. 3 × 1000 = 3000
11. 4 × 500 = 2000
12. 6 × 9000 = 54 000
13. 10 × 200 = 2000
14. 4 × 700 = 2800
15. 9 × 7000 = 63 000
16. 3 × 500 = 1500
17. 12 × 70 = 840
18. 11 × 6000 = 66 000
19. 3 × 60 = 180
20. 11 × 800 = 8800
21. 9 × 3000 = 27 000
22. 12 × 800 = 9600
23. 5 × 40 = 200
24. 6 × 6000 = 36 000
25. 5 × 500 = 2500
26. 1 × 80 = 80
27. 11 × 600 = 6600
28. 7 × 100 = 700
29. 10 × 10 = 1000
30. 2 × 9000 = 18 000
31. 5 × 100 = 500
32. 11 × 90 = 990
33. 9 × 400 = 3600
34. 12 × 8000 = 96 000
35. 8 × 70 = 560
36. 3 × 400 = 1200
37. 2 × 1000 = 2000
38. 11 × 5000 = 55 000
39. 4 × 600 = 2400
40. 9 × 80 = 720

85